Growth of Islamic Banking in Indonesia

Indonesia is the most populous Muslim country in the world. Taking into account its endowments and potential economic resources, the Islamic banking industry in Indonesia was expected to take on an important role in facilitating more financial resources and to contribute to the internationalization of the Islamic mode of financing, particularly in the Asia-Pacific region. However, the reality is far from the expectation. This book aims to clarify the causes and fundamental constraints leading to the extraordinarily low level of Indonesia's Islamic financial deepening.

The authors draw on the traditions of Institutional Economics which are concerned with the rules or mechanisms of creating the "incentive" and "threat" for economic players, because the rules (institutions) matter as the determinant for economic development and economic efficiency. This book offers a fairly new analytical lens by hypothesizing that Islamic banks must earn additional profit – which the authors coin as "Islamic bank rent" – to maintain their franchise value as prudent *Shari'ah*-compliant lenders when compared to conventional banks. The authors argue that insufficient provision of the Islamic bank rent opportunity may have cost Indonesia's Islamic banks the opportunity to learn and improve their skills and capacity for credit risk management. The book also offers evidence in support of implementing economic and affirmative policy necessary for incubating and developing the Islamic banking industry in Indonesia, and making Indonesia an international Islamic financial hub in the Asia-Pacific region.

This book will be a useful resource for policy-makers and researchers interested in Islamic banking in Indonesia.

Sigit Pramono is Chairman of SEBI School of Islamic Economics and Lecturer at the University of Indonesia, Indonesia.

Yasushi Suzuki is Professor at the Ritsumeikan Asia Pacific University, Japan.

Islamic Business and Finance Series
Series Editor: Ishaq Bhatti

There is an increasing need for western politicians, financiers, bankers, and indeed the western business community in general to have access to high quality and authoritative texts on Islamic financial and business practices. Drawing on expertise from across the Islamic world, this new series will provide carefully chosen and focused monographs and collections, each authored/edited by an expert in their respective field all over the world.

The series will be pitched at a level to appeal to middle and senior management in both the western and the Islamic business communities. For the manager with a western background the series will provide detailed and up-to-date briefings on important topics; for the academics, postgraduates, business communities, manager with western and an Islamic background the series will provide a guide to best practice in business in Islamic communities around the world, including Muslim minorities in the west and majorities in the rest of the world.

Awqaf-led Islamic Social Finance
Innovative Solutions to Modern Applications
Edited by Mohd Ma'Sum Billah

The Evolution of Interest and Debt
From Middle Ages to Modern Times
Edited by Murat Ustaoğlu and Ahmet İncekara

Growth of Islamic Banking in Indonesia
Theory and Practice
Sigit Pramono and Yasushi Suzuki

Islamic Monetary Economics
Finance and Banking in Contemporary Muslim Economies
Edited by Taha Eğri and Zeyneb Hafsa Orhan

For more information about this series, please visit: www.routledge.com/Islamic-Business-and-Finance-Series/book-series/ISLAMICFINANCE

Growth of Islamic Banking in Indonesia

Theory and Practice

Sigit Pramono and Yasushi Suzuki

Routledge
Taylor & Francis Group
LONDON AND NEW YORK

First published 2021
by Routledge
2 Park Square, Milton Park, Abingdon, Oxon OX14 4RN

and by Routledge
605 Third Avenue, New York, NY 10017

First issued in paperback 2022

Routledge is an imprint of the Taylor & Francis Group, an informa business

British Library Cataloguing in Publication Data
A catalogue record for this book is available from the British Library

Library of Congress Cataloging in Publication Data
Names: Pramono, Sigit, 1958– author. | Suzuki, Yasushi, 1963– author.
Title: Growth of Islamic banking in Indonesia : theory and practice /
Sigit Pramono and Yasushi Suzuki.
Description: New York : Routledge, 2021. | Series: Islamic business and
finance series | Includes bibliographical references and index. |
Identifiers: LCCN 2020029501 (print) | LCCN 2020029502 (ebook) |
ISBN 9780367219475 (hardback) | ISBN 9780429268946 (ebook)
Subjects: LCSH: Banks and banking–Indonesia. |
Banks and banking–Religious aspects–Islam. |
Banks and banking–Government policy–Indonesia.
Classification: LCC HG3304 .P644 2021 (print) |
LCC HG3304 (ebook) | DDC 332.109598–dc23
LC record available at https://lccn.loc.gov/2020029501
LC ebook record available at https://lccn.loc.gov/2020029502

ISBN 13: 978-0-367-64451-2 (pbk)
ISBN 13: 978-0-367-21947-5 (hbk)
ISBN 13: 978-0-429-26894-6 (ebk)

DOI: 10.4324/9780429268946

Typeset in Galliard
by Newgen Publishing UK

Contents

Figures

Tables

Foreword

Looking at the history of Islamic economics in Indonesia, the notion and aspiration of free interest (*riba* free) in financial intermediaries and profit-and-loss-sharing (PLS) business contracts have been widely recognized in the society for a long time. Dr Mohammad Hatta, one of the founding fathers and the first Vice President of the Republic of Indonesia, was considered a "substantive approach" proponent in viewing Islamic economic thought; however, he acknowledged that the implementation of free interest as the Islamic mode of financial intermediation had been practised voluntarily by the Indonesian people even before independence in 1945.

Obviously, considering its potential for economic endowment, including the largest Muslim population in the world, Indonesia is expected to be a magnet for the centre of growth for the Islamic finance and banking industry. The authors of the book conduct extensive analyses through the chapters to capture a number of crucial issues in the industry, by shedding analytical light on its genesis and socio-political context, the conceptualization of Islamic bank rent, the regulatory frameworks, and the recent economic realities and performance of Indonesia's Islamic banking industry.

It is my privilege to note that this book will refresh readers' notions of the government's (financial authority) role in developing the banking and financial industry. So far as the unfettered and free market does not always well-incubate and discipline the industry, the governmental initiative is expected to realize a sound banking and financial system which contributes to sustainable and inclusive growth in the nation. This book argues how well or poorly the Indonesian governmental initiative, through its banking – including Islamic banking – restructuring programme, contributes to economic development by reducing the "oligarchic financial market" condition.

Drawing on the Institutional Economics approach as an analytical tool, the authors attempt with academic rigour to analyse the dilemma faced by Indonesia's Islamic banks as well as the regulators, aiming to give readers a silver lining in the dilemma. I hope that readers will enjoy the silver lining together with the new perspectives delivered by this book, which will facilitate further debate in the development of a sound and healthy Islamic banking system in Indonesia. Lastly, I would like to take this opportunity to congratulate Dr Sigit Pramono,

SEBI School of Islamic Economics, Indonesia, and Prof. Dr Yasushi Suzuki, Ritsumeikan Asia Pacific University, Japan, for their great academic contributions.

Prof. Dr Dorodjatun Kuntjoro-Jakti
Emeritus Professor of Economics at the Faculty of Economics and Business, University of Indonesia
Formerly the Coordinating Minister for the Economy, Republic of Indonesia (2001–2004)

Foreword

I am delighted to write a few words for this excellent co-authored book written by Dr Sigit Pramono, SEBI School of Islamic Economics, Indonesia, and Prof. Dr Yasushi Suzuki, Ritsumeikan Asia Pacific University, Japan. The book is written with insightful, critical, and unlocking observations. I can sense from this book an intensity of the authors' commitment to analysing the growth of Islamic banking in Indonesia. This book attempts to examine the theoretical background and empirical data through an analytical lens of a relatively new concept of the "Islamic bank rent" approach to portraying the growth of Indonesia's Islamic banking industry, particularly in the period of 2004–2018. Their critical and original approach should be applauded.

One of the salient contributions of this book is to offer a bridge between the theories and practices of various problems faced by Indonesia's Islamic banking industry. I believe that the analyses and findings in this book will definitely lead to a significant debate among academic scholars as well as all the stakeholders of the Islamic finance industry. The authors shed an analytical light on a political element in the process of issuing and reviewing a *fatwa* by the *fatwa* authorities as a potential cause of the extraordinarily low penetration of Indonesia's Islamic banks. The authors attempt to bridge the gap between "idealists" and "pragmatists", seeking a consensus for prioritizing the pragmatist view on the "wealth creation first" strategy in the Islamic banking development programme.

I am more than happy to be given the great privilege to write a foreword for the book. I believe that all the practitioners and scholars of Islamic finance will find the book interesting and informative, and find it helpful in refreshing their views in Islamic finance. Finally, I would like to congratulate the authors as well as the publisher in conveying this inspiring book.

Datuk Dr Mohd Daud Bakar
President, International Islamic University of Malaysia (IIUM)
Founder and Executive Chairman, Amanie Group

Preface

Indonesia is the most populous Muslim country in the world and has abundant endowments and potential economic resources. The Islamic banking industry in Indonesia was expected to take an important role in facilitating more financial resources and to contribute as a magnet to the internationalization of the Islamic mode of financing in the Asia-Pacific region. However, the reality is far from the expectation. Indonesia's Islamic financial deepening stays at an extraordinarily low level with a market share of no more than 6 per cent of the total Indonesian banking industry at the end of 2018. Also, the slow-paced growth, particularly during the period of 2005 to 2018, has become a big concern for all the stakeholders in the Islamic banking industry, including the financial authorities and academics. We note that the slow-paced penetration of Islamic banking has reached the size of its total assets at IDR 477 trillion (equivalent to around USD 32 billion) as at the end of 2018. This size is counted as just around 2 per cent of global Islamic banking assets. How can we make sense of this extraordinarily low level of Islamic financial deepening and the slow-paced growth of Islamic banking in Indonesia?

The infrastructure of Islamic finance is necessary for facilitating investment and economic transactions by Muslim depositors and investors. If the infrastructure is not available, they would have to pay more transaction costs for *Shari'ah* compliance at individual levels. If they were aware (or unsure) that the proceeds from their investment had not complied with the *Shari'ah* principles, Muslim investors would consider the need for the proceeds to be "purified", for instance, by donating to charity or *zakat* institutions. This circumstance may discourage them from engaging in investment. In other words, the infrastructure of Islamic finance could possibly mobilize more funds from Muslim investors, which would also contribute to national economic growth. The governmental initiatives for developing the infrastructure of Islamic finance are expected to reduce the high transaction cost for *Shari'ah* compliance at the individual level. These initiatives are not only for the sake of Muslim investors, but also for society's, because if more funds from Muslim investors are mediated for investment, they would contribute to the growth of the nation.

While we acknowledge that Indonesia's Islamic banking industry was born and incubated by great efforts in various ways by the stakeholders of the industry, the penetration of Islamic banking is still marginal as of today. Taking into consideration the above mentioned macroeconomic impact, we have a different view from a "neoliberal" perspective, such that if the extraordinarily low level of Islamic financial penetration was the result of fair competition in the market, the redundant financial institutions had better leave the market. In our view, we should not leave Indonesia's Islamic banks as redundant financial institutions.

Drawing on the traditions of Institutional Economics which are concerned with the rules or mechanisms of creating the "incentive" and "threat" for economic players, we hypothesize that Islamic banks must earn the extra profit as earned by conventional banks – we call it "Islamic bank rent" – so that Islamic banks may maintain their franchise value as prudent *Shariah*-compliant lenders. We presume that insufficient provision of the Islamic bank rent opportunity may have lost Indonesia's Islamic banks the incentive to learn and to improve their skills and capacity for credit risk management. We point out that the Indonesian regulators failed to institutionalize a profit/rent opportunity to be captured by Islamic banks for the purpose of incubating the Indonesian Islamic banking industry, and failed to prepare a real level playing field with conventional banks in Indonesia.

This book sheds an analytical light on the history, regulatory framework, structural economic constraints, and distribution of political power in shaping and underpinning the establishment and development of the Islamic banking industry in Indonesia. This book offers an amount of evidence to support the leadership in implementing an economic and adequate affirmative policy by the financial authorities, which is a necessary condition, though we are not sure whether it is a sufficient condition for incubating and developing the Islamic banking industry in Indonesia and for making Indonesia an international Islamic financial hub in the Asia-Pacific region. While this may cause a controversy, we believe that the fairly new concept of Islamic bank rent as argued in this book would contribute to an academic debate on what is feasible for creating the harmonious co-existence of Islamic banking and conventional banking in Indonesia, which would benefit all the stakeholders of Islamic and conventional banking, accordingly.

Lastly, we acknowledge that Chapter 10 of this book has been added to propose a new theoretical framework as a reminder of the basic principles in Islamic law for making it easier (*taysir*) to remove people's unnecessary hardship (*raf 'al-haraj*) in the existing debate on the prohibition of *riba*. The original manuscript of this chapter was written by Yasushi Suzuki in *Islamic Civilization and Renewal* (2019, *10*(2), pp. 175–188), entitled "Riba, usury and Keynes". We believe that the framework offers a novel perspective on *murabaha*, and this would also lead to a significant debate in explaining the extraordinarily low level of Islamic banking penetration in Indonesia.

Sigit Pramono and Yasushi Suzuki
June 2020

Acknowledgements

The authors would like to thank Routledge/Taylor & Francis Asia Pacific for their guidance and continuous support towards the publication of this book.

Sigit Pramono would like to convey his heartiest gratitude to Prof. Dr Yasushi Suzuki for his immense encouragement, outstanding support, and continuous guidance to successfully complete this book project. He would also like to express his sincere gratitude to Rufidah Mansur and all our little angels for their everlasting love; without their help and cooperation this book may not have seen the light of day. He retains special thanks to all respected colleagues and students at SEBI School of Islamic Economics for their great help and inspiration for the academic work.

Yasushi Suzuki would like to acknowledge that his work was supported by JSPS Grant-in-Aid for Scientific Research (C), Grant Number 19K01749. He would like to thank Akiko Suzuki for her constant support. Several years of the Finance and Economics postgraduate seminar members, including Dr Sigit Pramono, at Ritsumeikan Asia Pacific University incubated some arguments in this book. Their enthusiasm, support, comments, and criticism were invaluable.

The authors would like to convey their highest gratitude and appreciation to Prof. Dr Dorodjatun Kuntjoro-Jakti and Datuk Dr Mohd Daud Bakar for their kindness and encouragement; also, for all respected colleagues and institutions who, in their own ways, have helped us in this academic work.

1 Introduction

1. Introduction

Since the launch of the economic "Islamization" movement through the experimental establishment of Islamic financial institutions in the 1970s, Islamic finance has attracted global attention. In fact, Islamic banking and finance have rapidly and vigorously expanded in the past four decades (Sardar, 1988; Iqbal and Mirakhor, 2007; Ismal, 2011, 2013). In the first half of 2014, the global Islamic finance industry accounted for total assets amounting to USD 1.87 trillion and had recorded a double-digit compound annual growth rate of 17 per cent between 2009 and 2013. Later, the Islamic Financial Service Board's *Islamic Financial Services Industry (IFSI) Stability Report 2019* (IFSB, 2019) reported a continuous improvement in the global Islamic financial industry during 2015–2018. Noticeably, its total worth had reached USD 2.19 trillion in the first half of 2018. It is evident that the banking sector is the dominant segment in the global Islamic financial industry. Global Islamic banking assets (covering fully-fledged Islamic banks, subsidiaries, and *Shari'ah* windows) amounted to about USD 1.48 trillion and shared about 79 per cent of the global Islamic finance assets in mid-2014 (IFSB, 2015). In 2018, the Islamic banking sector had attained USD 1.57 trillion and contributed to approximately 71.7 per cent of the total assets of the global Islamic financial industry (IFSB, 2019).

In Indonesia, the country which is reported to have the largest Muslim population, the market share of Islamic banks stayed at no more than 6 per cent of the total Indonesian banking industry during the period from 2004 to 2018 (FSA, 2015a–2019a). As we see later, compared to the other Muslim countries, Indonesia's Islamic financial deepening is at an extraordinarily low level, despite it having the largest Muslim population. In addition, we note the slow-paced penetration of Islamic banking in reaching the size of its total assets at IDR 477 trillion (equivalent to around USD 32 billion) as at the end of 2018. This size is counted as just around 2 per cent of global Islamic banking assets. How can we make sense of this low level of Islamic financial deepening and the slow-paced growth of Islamic banking in Indonesia given that the country has the largest Muslim population in the world? The total population of Indonesia was estimated at 204.8 million people and the Muslim proportion was about 88.1

per cent in 2010 (Pew Research Center, 2011). Nonetheless, in terms of banking market share in Indonesia, Islamic banking has been stagnant with a share of only 1.2 to 5.9 per cent during the period from 2004 to 2018 (Sukmana and Kuswanto, 2015; FSA, 2015–2019; 2015a–2019a).

The market penetration of Islamic banking in Indonesia stays at a very low level. Also, the slow-paced growth (particularly during the period from 2005 to 2018) has become a big concern for all the stakeholders, including the banking regulator, of the Islamic banking industry, because the banking sector is, in general, a highly regulated industry. In fact, some important initiatives have been conducted by the government to facilitate the development of Islamic banking. The regulatory process of ratification for financial products has provided a legal framework for the purpose of enhancing the Islamic financial market. For instance, the enactment of the Islamic Banking Act No. 21 of 2008 aimed to increase legal assurance and trust for the stakeholders on the products and services of Islamic banking and finance in Indonesia. Besides, there are several regulations aiming to facilitate the development of Indonesia's Islamic banks, including Act No. 38 Year 1999 on *Zakat*; Act No. 41 Year 2004 on *Waqf* (Islamic Endowment); Act No. 24 Year 2004 on *Lembaga Penjamin Simpanan* (Deposit Insurance Corporation); Act No. 3 Year 2006 on *Peradilan Agama* (Religious Court); Act No. 40 Year 2007 on *Perseroan Terbatas* (Limited Company); and Act No. 19 Year 2008 on *Surat Berharga Syariah Negara* (SBSN, *Sukuk* Act). The financial regulator – the Financial Services Authority (FSA) – is worried about the slow-paced growth of Islamic banking in Indonesia. In a strategic paper entitled *Roadmap of Indonesian Islamic Banking 2015–2019*, the FSA (2015) launched a vision for "actualizing Islamic banking that gives significant contributions to sustainable economic growth, equitable development, financial system stability, and has high competitiveness". This vision was embodied in seven policy directions, work programmes, and a schedule to be comprehensively implemented in the timeframe of 2015 to 2019 (FSA, 2015, pp. xv–xvi). Still, the impact of Islamic banking on Indonesian economy is not significant at this point in writing.

Even though Indonesia has the largest Muslim population, and despite the fact that the regulatory initiatives have been implemented for the purpose of facilitating the Islamic banking industry, why is the Islamic financial deepening (the market share of Islamic banks) extraordinarily low? What are the root causes of this stagnation in Islamic banking? What has caused the recent trend of slow-paced Islamic financial deepening? Is this trend related to the Islamic banks' performance on operational efficiency? We call these questions "Puzzle 1" in this book. The main purpose of this book is to solve this puzzle.

To tackle Puzzle 1, we are going to look at the case of Malaysia, a close neighbouring Muslim country that has somewhat successfully proceeded with the Islamization of its own banking industry. What were the secrets for the successful development of Malaysia's Islamic banking? How well (or poorly) can Malaysia's Islamic financial architecture be applied to Indonesia? How do the stakeholders of Islamic banks in Indonesia interact and resolve "the structural dilemma" faced by the Indonesian Islamic banking industry (especially the FSA, Bank Indonesia (BI, the central bank), the government of Indonesia, and the bankers)? How did they fail to manage the market and institutional/state alignments with the process of the Islamization of banking industry under the dual banking system? We call these questions "Puzzle 2". We aim to draw the policy options for Indonesia to bail its Islamic banking out of the above-mentioned stagnant situation, mainly through comparison with the case of Malaysia.

2. Arguments in the existing literature and research gaps

Several approaches have attempted to explain the low level of Islamic financial deepening and the recent trend of slow-paced growth in Indonesian Islamic banking. As Abduh and Omar (2012) insist, economic growth is a major factor that determines the development of Islamic banking. However, we should ask why Indonesia's Islamic banking has stagnated while its conventional banking has been expanding under the same economic circumstances.

One explanation is that customers' preferences and saving behaviour are a critical factor that can determine the development of Islamic banking. Kasri and Kassim (2009) investigated Indonesian Islamic banks' customer behaviour in placing their deposits. They investigated the real rate of return on Islamic deposits, the interest rate on conventional deposits, and the real income and number of Islamic bank branches as the factors which determine the level of savings in Islamic banks. Kasri and Kassim found that the level of Islamic bank deposits is positively correlated with the rate of return on Islamic deposits and negatively correlated with the rate of interest offered by conventional banks if Islamic banks fail to follow it. This is the "displaced commercial risk" by "rational Muslim depositors' behaviour" (ibid., 2009).

This is a strong counterargument to Lindsey (2012), who insists that the initiatives are predominantly aimed at co-opting the Muslim community – for whom the excellence of *Shari'ah* compliance matters – as their potential customers. The rational Muslim depositors' behaviour hypothesis, however, does not fully explain the low level of Islamic financial deepening, because Indonesia's Islamic banks seem to attract their depositors by offering a rate that is still competitive with that offered by conventional banks, as discussed in Chapter 3.

Some other scholars are concerned about public awareness of Islamic banking services as the key factor in fostering the growth of Islamic banks in Indonesia (Zubair, 2008; Ismal, 2014). Sari et al. (2016) point out the lack of trust among consumers and the overall consumer misunderstanding of Islamic banking; it seems that public awareness for filling in the gaps would be necessary for the growth of Indonesia's Islamic banking industry. In other words, they point out that Indonesia's Islamic banks are still "infant", resulting in a failure of installing sufficient confidence and trust in Islamic banking to compete with conventional banks. However, these approaches do not sufficiently explain why Indonesia's Islamic banks are still infant and what caused the recent trend of low Islamic financial deepening.

Lai (2015) attempts to justify the Malaysian governmental initiative of incubating infant Islamic banks under a protective financial architecture. This was done to strengthen Malaysia's position as a leading player in the international financial hub by contributing to the globalization of Islamic financial industry. However, this argument does not sufficiently address how to measure the economic benefit of the protective financial architecture and does not clearly mention until when the protection should last.

In order to fill in the lacuna in the existing literature, we believe that it is necessary to shed an analytical light on the institutional inefficiency which may have failed to create appropriate "incentive" and "threat" in the banking operations by Indonesian Islamic banks. We draw on the traditions of New Institutional Economics (NIE), which are concerned about the rules or mechanisms of creating the incentive and threat to economic players, in order to provide a theoretical framework for tackling the above-mentioned puzzles. NIE assumes that economic institutions would matter as a determinant for economic development and economic efficiency. We are particularly concerned about the regulatory framework (formal institution) which creates the "financial sector rent" (bank rent (surplus) opportunity) to be captured by banks as the incentive for making them become prudent fund providers (Hellman et al., 1997; Khan, 2000; Suzuki, 2011; Suzuki and Uddin, 2014). We will discuss the bank rent theory in Chapter 4.

Although some studies have discussed the issue related to the slow growth in Indonesian Islamic banks, this book aims to argue the phenomenon by presenting new angles, such as: (1) how well (or poorly) the "Islamic bank rent opportunity" is used by Islamic banks to maintain their franchise value and reputation; and (2) how the regulators (FSA, BI, and Government of Indonesia) failed to create the adequate incentive mechanism (i.e. the maintenance of constrained/moderate competition level) for Islamic banks, consequently resulting in excessive competition and general inefficiency in their operation.

3. Hypotheses and methodology

This book aims to clarify the reasons or fundamental constraints behind the low level of Islamic financial deepening in Indonesia. Also, it strives to make sense of the recent trend of slow-paced credit expansion by Indonesian Islamic banks. In addition, this research provides an overview of the regulatory framework on which the operation of Indonesian Islamic banks is based, and the recent performance of Islamic banking development in Indonesia.

We hypothesize the following: (1) Indonesia's Islamic banks are not given an adequate incentive (including rent opportunity) for contributing to Islamic financial deepening. In other words, the financial regulators (BI and FSA) failed to create an adequate incentive for Islamic banks in Indonesia, leading to a state failure of omission; (2) owing to the "severe" competition with conventional banks (also among Islamic banks) in the banking industry, Islamic banks cannot afford to earn sufficient profits for maintaining their franchise value and reputation. At the same time, while Islamic banks have to deal with the unique risks such as the displacement risk (due to *Shari'ah* non-compliance) and/or the credit risk and uncertainty upon the profit-and-loss-sharing (PLS) agreement, the tight competition, particularly in the market for consumer financing, does not allow Islamic banks to earn the "Islamic bank rent" to absorb the above-mentioned unique risks.

In order to test the above hypotheses and tackle Puzzle 1, we develop our methods as follows:

1. We review the genesis and development of Indonesian regulatory policy for incubating Islamic banks to clarify the features (or constraints) in the Indonesian policy for the Islamization of its banking industry. We compare it with Malaysia's regulatory policy for incubating Islamic banks.
2. We investigate the profitability and stability of Indonesian Islamic banks compared to conventional banks. We hypothesize that Indonesian Islamic banks are not given an adequate incentive (rent opportunity) for contributing to their credit expansion. We collect and analyse the financial statements of major Islamic/conventional banks in Indonesia. We follow the concept of "Islamic bank rent" proposed by Suzuki and Uddin (2014), in which Islamic banks must earn an extra profit (the Islamic bank rent) to maintain their franchise value as prudent *Shari'ah*-compliant lenders, by absorbing peculiar risks and uncertainty embedded in the mode of PLS. We hypothesize that the low level of Indonesian Islamic financial deepening is the result of a failure to create appropriate extra profits to be captured by Islamic banks.
3. We hypothesize that "severe" competition with conventional banks may have hampered the opportunity to expand their operation by Islamic banks. We hypothesize that the competition has recently been intensified, particularly since 2012. To test the hypothesis, we are going to: (i) review the credit portfolios of Islamic banks and conventional banks to see how their customers and domains are overlapping (i.e. how they are competing); (ii) assess how the concentration and competition level has been changed in the banking sector in Indonesia. We apply two concentration measurement methods: *k*-bank concentration ratio and Herfindahl-Hirschman Index, a detailed explanation of which is provided in Chapter 7; (iii) conduct interviews with Islamic bank managers as a qualitative analysis to clarify what has happened since 2008 in credit policy and portfolio, particularly in major Islamic banks.
4. We also analyse how the operational efficiency in Islamic banks has been improving or deteriorating. We employ data envelopment analysis for estimating the changes in the level of efficiency, which will be detailed in Chapter 8. It is reported that Indonesian Islamic banks maintain a portfolio of *musharaka* (equity-like participatory financing), while Islamic banks in other countries have fallen into the so-called *murabaha* (asset-based financing or hire purchase) syndrome. This book analyses the reality of their credit portfolio in Islamic banks to seek a reason or constraint for the recent trend

of slowdown in their banking operations. The above-mentioned qualitative methods are also used for the analysis.

Also, we develop our methods to tackle Puzzle 2 as follows:

1. This research sheds light on the historical, socio-economic, and socio-political background of the genesis of Islamic banks in Indonesia to understand the Indonesian Islamic banking landscape, which is characterized as a dual – not centralized – banking regime. In addition, we compare it with the case of Malaysia to clarify the reason for Malaysia's successful transformation (Islamization) of the banking industry, then to clarify the reason behind the stagnant transformation in Indonesia. We hypothesize that while a positive "rent effect" in terms of seeking economies of scale for branch network expansion was observed in Malaysia, the rent opportunity to be captured by Indonesian Islamic banks was not enough to achieve the adequate economies of scale.
2. Through the comparative study of regulatory frameworks between Indonesia and Malaysia, we attempt to clarify why the Indonesian banking regulator(s) failed to incubate Islamic banks by not giving them a learning rent opportunity or designing a level playing field between conventional and Islamic banks in an appropriate timeframe. We investigate the secret of Malaysia's effective state intervention to successfully incubate its Islamic banking industry.

Figure 1.1 illustrates the flow of analysis in tackling the two puzzles. To tackle Puzzle 1, we test Hypothesis 1 mainly through the discussions in Chapters 2, 3, 4, 6, and 10. Then, we test Hypothesis 2 in Chapter 7. To tackle Puzzle 2, in Chapters 5 and 8 we test the hypothesis that while a positive rent effect is observed in Malaysia, it is not observed in Indonesia. In this context, it is arguable whether Indonesian Islamic banks need to earn an extra profit – Islamic bank rent, in the term adopted by Suzuki and Uddin (2014) – to maintain their franchise value as prudent *Shari'ah*-compliant lenders, since they have to deal with the unique risk and uncertainty in their operations based upon the PLS mode. In Chapter 9 we look at the structural dilemma in Indonesia's Islamic banking industry, drawing on the approach of Khan (2000), to clarify why the Indonesian banking regulator(s) failed to incubate Islamic banks. Suzuki and Uddin (2014) suggest that Islamic banks must earn an extra risk-adjusted premium covering the measurable risk, as commonly charged also by the conventional banks, plus the Islamic bank rent to compensate for the unique risk and uncertain challenges faced by Islamic banks. One of the implications is that it would be difficult to design a level playing field for both Islamic and conventional banks.

We collected primary data through in-depth interviews with the banking regulators in Indonesia (BI and FSA), Islamic bankers (senior managers or directors) in Indonesia and Malaysia, academic scholars (lecturers/researchers at universities or research institutions) in Indonesia and Malaysia, and senior officers

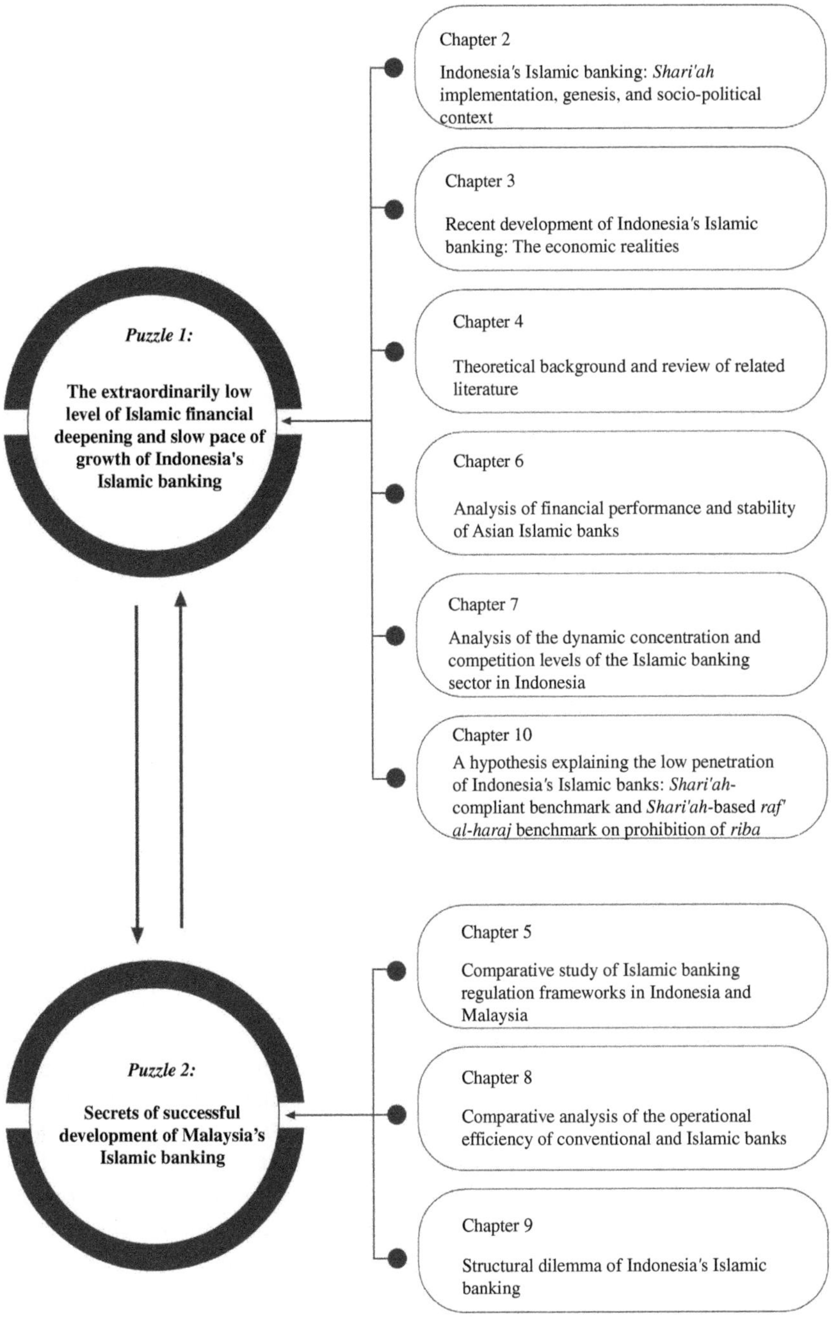

Figure 1.1 The flow of analysis in tackling the puzzles.
Source: Constructed by the authors.

of the Ministry of State Owned Enterprises of the Republic of Indonesia. We conducted unstructured interviews based upon the qualitative analysis method of Eisenhardt and Bourgeois (1988) as well as Patton (2002), mainly because we think that the unstructured method helps the interviewer to have non-standardized questions and in-depth explorations into the topic.

Meanwhile, we collected secondary data mainly from the annual reports and/or financial statements of 14 fully-fledged Islamic commercial banks and 20 Islamic banking windows in Indonesia as of December 2018. Also, we collected a series of regulations and announcements issued by the regulators, particularly during the period from 2003 to 2018. For the above-mentioned comparative analysis, we collected the financial data of randomly selected Islamic banks and conventional banks in Malaysia and Bangladesh.

4. Chapter outline

Chapter 2 gives an overview of the birth and initial development of Islamic banking in the context of the social, political, and economic dimensions in Indonesia in order to initiate the tackling of Puzzle 1. This chapter also presents the dynamics of *fatwa* (*Shari'ah* or Islamic legal opinion) on the prohibition of bank interest in Indonesia issued by the main *fatwa* authorities in Indonesia. Chapter 3 presents the recent development of Indonesian Islamic banking in the period from 2004 to 2018. In this chapter we analyse the current performance of Indonesia's Islamic banks.

We observe in Chapter 3 the lower profitability performance and the deteriorating trend of financial performance indicators of Indonesian Islamic banks in comparison with those of conventional banks during the period between 2005 and 2018. In the theoretical framework of the "financial restraint" policy (Hellman et al., 1997), which creates the financial sector rent opportunity as the incentives for prudent fund providers, a bank must earn enough profit to maintain its franchise value and reputation by reducing potential information problems such as moral hazard and adverse selection. The ability to generate profits and accumulate capital in the long run, in turn, would enable the bank to expand its banking business through the expansion of branch networks (this is considered a positive rent effect). Furthermore, the positive rent effect would contribute to ensuring a sound banking system, which in turn would increase the financial deepening level in the economy in the end (Hellman et al., 1997; Suzuki and Adhikary, 2009; Suzuki, 2011; Wanniarachchige, 2017). Chapter 4 develops our theoretical framework, in which we draw on the theoretical framework of financial sector rent (bank rent) to justify the creation of rent (surplus) opportunity to be captured by banks as the incentive for making them become prudent fund providers (Hellmann, et al., 1997; Khan, 2000; Suzuki, 2011; Suzuki and Uddin, 2014).

Chapter 5 provides a comparative study of Islamic banking regulatory frameworks between Indonesia and Malaysia. Chapter 6 presents a comparative analysis of financing activities and financial performance indicators of Islamic banking operations in Indonesia, Malaysia, and Bangladesh. In this chapter, we look at the *murabaha* syndrome faced by Islamic banks in these three countries. This chapter analyses the unique practice in the mode of financing Indonesian Islamic banks, in which the credit portfolio under *mudaraba/musharaka* contracts is relatively high in comparison to the credit assets practised by Islamic banks in Malaysia and Bangladesh.

Chapter 7 analyses the dynamic concentration and competition levels in the banking sector of Indonesia. Chapter 8 provides a comparative analysis of the operational efficiency between Islamic banks and conventional banks in Indonesia by discussing the rent effect brought about by Islamic banks in Indonesia. The discussion is supported by the review of empirical results of the efficiency level of Malaysian Islamic banks.

Chapter 9 discusses the structural dilemma in Indonesia's Islamic banking industry and the process of institutional (state) failure to incubate Indonesian Islamic banks. Chapter 10 proposes a new theoretical framework as a reminder of the basic principles in Islamic law for making it easier (*taysir*) to remove people's unnecessary hardship (*raf' al-haraj*) in the existing debate on the prohibition of *riba*. This chapter points out that Indonesia's Islamic banking might be trapped in a "diminishing equilibrium" upon strict *Shari'ah* compliance, which would explain the phenomenon of the low penetration of Indonesian Islamic banks. Finally, Chapter 11 presents an epilogue to summarize our findings and proposes some policy options for empowering Indonesia's Islamic banking industry.

References

Abduh, M. and Omar, M.A. (2012) Islamic banking and economic growth: The Indonesian experience, *International Journal of Islamic and Middle Eastern Finance and Management*, *5*(1), pp. 35–47.

Eisenhardt, K.M. and Bourgeois, L.J. (1988) Politics of strategic decision-making in high-velocity environments – toward a midrange theory, *Academy of Management Journal*, *31*, pp. 737–770.

Financial Services Authority (FSA). (2015) *Roadmap of Indonesian Islamic Banking 2015–2019* (*Roadmap Perbankan Syariah Indonesia 2015–2019*). Jakarta: FSA, Republic of Indonesia.

Financial Services Authority (FSA). (2015–2019) *Indonesian Banking Statistics December 2014–2018*. Jakarta: FSA, Republic of Indonesia.

Financial Services Authority (FSA). (2015a–2019a) *Indonesian Islamic Banking Statistics December 2014–2018*. Jakarta: FSA, Republic of Indonesia.

Hellmann, T., Murdock, K., and Stiglitz, J. (1997) Financial restraint: Toward a new paradigm, in M. Aoki, H.-K. Kim, and M. Okuno-Fujiwara (Eds) *The Role of Government in East Asian Economic Development: Comparative Institutional Analysis*. Oxford: Clarendon Press, pp. 163–207.

Iqbal, Z. and Mirakhor, A. (2007) *An Introduction to Islamic Finance, Theory and Practice*. Singapore: John and Wiley & Sons.

Islamic Financial Service Board (IFSB). (2015) *IFSB's Islamic Financial Services Industry* (*IFSI*) *Stability Report 2015*. Kuala Lumpur: IFSB.

Islamic Financial Service Board (IFSB). (2019) *IFSB's Islamic Financial Services Industry (IFSI) Stability Report 2019*. Kuala Lumpur: IFSB.

Ismal, R. (2011) Islamic banking in Indonesia: Lessons learnt. Paper presented at *Multi-Year Expert Meeting on Services, Development and Trade: The Regulatory and Institutional Dimension*, Geneva, 6–8 April 2011.

Ismal, R. (2013) *Islamic Banking in Indonesia: New Perspectives on Monetary and Financial Issues*. Singapore: John Wiley and Sons.

Ismal, R. (2014) Indonesia, the resilience and prospects of Islamic banking, in S. Thiagaraja et al. (Eds) *The Islamic Finance Handbook, A Practitioner's Guide to the Global Market*. Singapore: John Wiley & Sons, pp. 155–173.

Kasri, R.A. and Kassim S.H. (2009) Empirical determinants of saving in the Islamic banks: Evidence from Indonesia, *Islamic Economics, 22*(2), pp. 3–23.

Khan, M.H. (2000) Rents, efficiency and growth, in M.H. Khan and J.K. Sundaram (Eds) *Rents, Rent-seeking and Economic Development: Theory and Evidence in Asia*. Cambridge: Cambridge University Press, pp. 21–69.

Lai, J. (2015) Industrial policy and Islamic finance, *New Political Economy, 20*(2), pp. 178–198.

Lindsey, T. (2012) Between piety and prudence: State Syariah and the regulation of Islamic banking in Indonesia, *Sydney Law Review, 34*(107), pp. 1–16.

Patton, M.Q. (2002) *Qualitative Research and Evaluation Methods*. Thousand Oaks, CA: Sage.

Pew Research Center. (2011) The future of the global Muslim population: Projections for 2010–2030. Retrieved from: http://assets.pewresearch.org/wpcontent/uploads/sites/11/2011/01/FutureGlobalMuslimPopulationWebPDF-Feb10.pdf

Sardar, Z. (1988) *Islamic Futures: The Shape of Ideas to Come*. Kuala Lumpur: Pelanduk Publication.

Sari, M.D., Bahari, Z., and Hamat, Z. (2016) History of Islamic Bank in Indonesia: Issues behind its establishment, *International Journal of Finance and Banking Research, 2*(5), pp. 178–184. doi: 10.11648/j.ijfbr.20160205.13

Sukmana, R. and Kuswanto, H. (2015) Assessment on the Islamic banking market share projection by Bank Indonesia and proposed methods, *Journal of Islamic Monetary Economics and Finance, 1*(1), pp. 107–133.

Suzuki, Y. (2011) *Japan's Financial Slump: Collapse of the Monitoring System under Institutional and Transition Failures*. London: Palgrave Macmillan.

Suzuki, Y. and Adhikary, B. K. (2009) A "Bank Rent" approach to understanding the development of the banking system in Bangladesh, *Contemporary South Asia, 18*(2), pp. 155–173.

Suzuki, Y. and Uddin, S.M.S. (2014) Islamic bank rent: A case study of Islamic banking in Bangladesh, *International Journal of Islamic and Middle Eastern Finance and Management, 7*(2), pp. 170–181.

Wanniarachchige, M.K. (2017) Creating bank rent in developing countries: An integrated model', in Y. Suzuki, M.D. Miah, M.K. Wanniarachchige, and S.M.S. Uddin (Eds) *Banking and Economic Rent in Asia: Rent Effects, Financial Fragility, and Economic Development*. Abingdon, UK: Routledge, pp. 38–57.

Zubair, M.K. (2008) Acceleration of the growth of Islamic banking in Indonesia. *Journal Millah, 8*(1), pp. 1–19.

2 Indonesia's Islamic banking

Shari'ah implementation, genesis, and socio-political context

1. Introduction

Our discussion in this chapter aims to present an overview of the birth and initial development of Indonesian Islamic banking. This chapter sheds an analytical light on the implementation of *Shari'ah* in the economy, and looks at the genesis and the social-political context of Indonesia's Islamic banking. The rest of this chapter is organized as follows. To begin with, the implementation of *Shari'ah* as the root of Islamic banking operation is discussed in Section 2. Section 3 brings our discussion to the *fatwa* (*Shari'ah* or Islamic legal opinion) on the prohibition of *riba* (interest) in Indonesia. Then, Section 4 presents a historical background of the genesis as the initial development of Islamic banking in Indonesia. In addition, this section also provides a brief discussion of the economic Islamization movement in the Muslim world. Subsequently, an extensive discussion of the socio-political context of Islamic banking in Indonesia is presented in Section 5.

2. *Shari'ah* implementation in the economy

In principle, Islam, as the religion revealed by Allah the Almighty, consists of three grand rules as a comprehensive guidance to all aspects of Muslim life (Laldin, 2007; Antonio, 2010; Ismal, 2013). First is the aspect of *Aqidah* that carries out the fundamental relationship between God and His creatures (the sanctions relating to beliefs). Second, *Shari'ah* is the manifestation aspect of the beliefs (the sanctions relating to God's laws). Third, *Akhlaq* is the moral aspect, which provides the attitude and ethics guidance for humankind (the sanctions relating to morals and ethics). For Muslims, it means that the principles of Islamic teachings should be transformed from normative values into a set of factual concepts (Achsien, 2000). Muslims should follow these Islamic teachings as a comprehensive way of life.

The word *Shari'ah* is derived from its roots of *shin*, *ra*, and *'ayn* in Arabic letters. Literally, the meaning of *Shari'ah* is "the road to the watering place, the straight path to be followed" (Laldin, 2007, p. 6). Referring to this linguistic meaning, *Shari'ah* can be interpreted as the canon law of Islam or divine injunction that should be followed by individual and collective lives, and which will direct human life onto the right path (Laldin, 2007, p. 6; Ayub, 2007, p. 21; Lee and Detta, 2007, p. 41).

It is also meaningful to understand that *Shari'ah* is built on a foundation that emphasizes the welfare of the people in this world as well as in the hereafter, as written by classical Islamic scholar Ibn Qayyim al-Jawziyyah (died 1350 CE) in his book *I'lam al-Muwaqqi'in* (see Chapra, 1992, p. 1):

> *The basis of the Shari'ah is wisdom and welfare of the people in this world as well as the Hereafter. This welfare lies in complete justice, mercy, well-being and wisdom. Anything that departs from justice to oppression, from mercy to harshness, from welfare to misery and from wisdom to folly, has nothing to do with the Shari'ah.*

The *Shari'ah*, as the tools of do's and don'ts in Islamic law, consists of two basic elements: (1) rituals (*Ibadah*), by which people worship God; and (2) relationships and dealings between humans and other creatures (*Muamalah*), including the way in which humans perform their economic and non-economic activities in their lives (Achsien, 2000; Antonio, 2010; Ismal, 2013). In this regard, we acknowledge the Islamic jurisprudence that covers the rulings to govern the relationship between humans and Allah the Almighty as *Fiqh al Ibadah*; whereas the Islamic jurisprudence that covers the rulings to govern the relationship between humans, and other creatures of Allah the Almighty, as *Fiqh al Muamalah* (Laldin, 2007). Figure 2.1 illustrates the position of *Shari'ah* in a comprehensive view of Islamic teaching.

The main purpose of *Shari'ah* is explained by classical Islamic scholar Abu Hamid Al-Ghazali (died 1111 CE) in his famous book *Al Mustasfa* (see Chapra, 2000, p. 118):

> *The objective of the Shari'ah is to promote the well-being of all mankind, which lies in safeguarding their faith (al-dien), their human self (al-nafs), their intellect (al-'aql), their posterity (al-nasl), and their wealth (al-mal). Whatever ensures the safeguard of these five serves public interest and is desirable.*

In brief, we see that the primary purpose of the implementation of *Shari'ah* (known as *Maqashid al Shari'ah*) in human life is closely related to the concept of *maslahah* (public interest or benefit) and it is, *inter alia*, to realize socio-economic justice and preserve wellbeing for all God's creatures in this world and the hereafter.

3. The *fatwa* (*Shari'ah* opinion) on the prohibition of *riba* (interest) in Indonesia

Shari'ah can be regarded as the guidance source of Islamic economic contracts, particularly the *Shari'ah-Muamalah* principles. In relating to contemporary Islamic banking development, we outline below the basic principles which

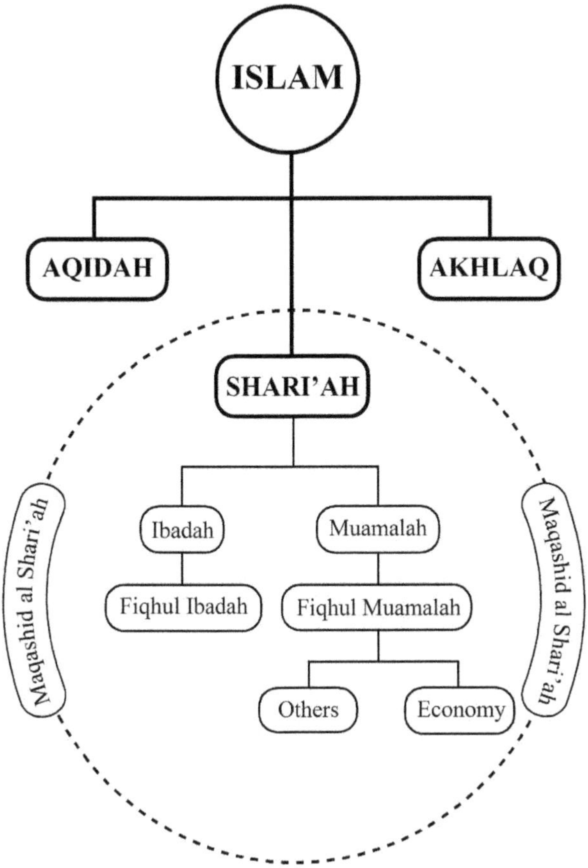

Figure 2.1 The positioning of *Shari'ah* in a comprehensive view of Islam.

Source: Constructed by the authors based on Laldin (2007), Antonio (2010), and Ismal (2013).

provide the economic transactions guidance from the *Shari'ah* perspective (see Ainley et al., 2007; Ismal, 2013; Abojeib et al., 2018).

Firstly, Islam strongly encourages and recognizes the right of every individual to achieve personal economic wellbeing, while *Shari'ah* provides the clear guidelines and limitations as to what kinds of commercial activity are allowed or prohibited. For example, while Islam encourages individuals to engage in economic and business-related activities, particular businesses – in alcohol, swine, gambling, pornography, and other socially detrimental actions – are prohibited.

Secondly, one of the *Shari'ah* principles in economic activities is the prohibition of *riba* (interest/usury). Included in this category is contracting interest payments typically observed in the conventional credit agreement as one type of *riba* – predetermined profit on loans. Through the long history of scholarly discourses in the Muslim world, there surely exists a prevailing consensus among Muslim scholars that usury (*riba*) is unquestionably prohibited based on Islamic teaching (Chapra, 2000). However, in the context of the modern economy along with complex economic transactions, the issue on how to reach a consensus of defining what is meant by *riba* is still controversial, even among Muslim jurists.

As Chapra (2000) admits, while the western mode of finance using "interest" as a tool of reflecting and quantifying various risks has been dominant in the global financial market since colonialization by western countries, the Muslim world has been challenging this by attempting to introduce the Islamic mode of finance without using *riba*. However, some scholars and jurists wonder if the interest practised in modern banking is not necessarily the same as *riba*, which had existed in the pre-Islamic period. The proponents of this view insist that there is a need to review the meaning of *riba* in the context of contemporary economies. In fact, the controversy about the prohibition of *riba* has become one of the most critical issues in Islamic jurisprudence (Ceiro, 2004). According to Ceiro (2004), three positions of understanding of the prohibition of *riba* are identified: idealistic, liberal, and pragmatic. First, in the idealistic position, the "idealists" argue that interest is definitely *riba* and charging it should be regarded as a grave sin. According to the idealistic view, Islamic banks should design all of their business contracts in accordance with the classical and conservative interpretation of Islamic laws. In contrast, in the liberal- or *maslahah*-oriented position, the "liberalists" opine that since the concept of interest in banking does not necessarily correspond to the pre-Islamic *riba,* the interest applied in banking is not considered as the *riba* which is prohibited as a sin. The "pragmatists" stay or swing in between these two positions. This pragmatic position may have supported the evolution of contemporary Islamic banking. The pragmatists admit that the interest in banking is *riba* and thus, in general, prohibited. On the other hand, they propose that the efforts to overcome this controversy in pragmatic ways are necessary to develop the Islamic mode of banking.

We can see the pragmatic ways to develop Indonesia's Islamic banking industry by tracing the dynamics of *fatwa* on the prohibition of bank interest in Indonesia. In this country, three main Islamic organizations are acknowledged to have the authority to make *fatwa* and are considered as the foremost reference for the Indonesian community and government regarding legal issues in Islam. They are, namely, Lajnah Bahsul Masa'il, Nahdlatul Ulama (NU), Lembaga Tarjih, Muhammadiyah, and Majelis Ulama Indonesia (MUI, Indonesian Ulama Council). We can trace the dynamic and dialectical efforts by these *fatwa* authorities in the discourses and debates on the prohibition of bank interest in Indonesia.

It is worth noting that Lajnah Bahsul Masa'il, NU had reviewed three stances on the prohibition of bank interest at the second NU conference in Surabaya in 1927. The first view insisted that charging interest should be prohibited completely. The second suggested that bank interest was justifiable because of the difficulty in explicitly proving *ribawi* transactions in the contract of banking;

and the third categorized it as a doubtful economic transaction (*musytabihat*). Lajnah Bahsul Masa'il, NU underlined the importance of being cautious about this matter. The conference finally gave preference to the first view on the prohibition of bank interest, although the other opinions on the prohibition of interest were also accommodated.

Almost 40 years later, at a conference held by Lembaga Tarjih, Muhammadiyah, which took place in Sidoarjo on 23–27 July 1968, the organization cast doubt on the practice of bank interest charged by state-owned banks and categorized it as a dubious transaction (*musytabihat*). Accordingly, Lembaga Tarjih, Muhammadiyah recommended that the Central Board of Muhammadiyah should take the initiative for ensuring the economic and banking system was in line with Islamic principles. Still, on 21–25 January 1992, in a hearing to review legal considerations related to bank interest held by Lajnah Bahsul Masa'il, NU, the organization recommended that Islamic banking in Indonesia should be urgently established, though there was still controversy on the prohibition of bank interest, particularly among *fuqoha* (jurists) from NU.

On 24 January 2004, *Fatwa* No. 1 of 2004 concerning interest (*Fa'idah*/usury) was formally issued by MUI. We should note that even though this *fatwa* explicitly states that bank interest is prohibited, Decision No. 3 of this *fatwa* in the section "Business dealings (*Muamalah*) with conventional financial institutions" provides an exception, stating that: "For the areas where there is no network of Islamic Financial Institutions, it is permissible to conduct transaction activities in conventional financial institutions based on the principle of emergency (*dharuriyah*)".

Subsequently, on 18 June 2006, Majelis Tarjih, Muhammadiyah officially issued a *fatwa* on the prohibition of bank interest. Essentially, this particular *fatwa* can be perceived as a manifestation of Muhammadiyah members' aspiration in supporting the development of Islamic banking.

Consequently, the three *fatwa* authorities in Indonesia have come to take the same position on the prohibition of *riba* based upon the Islamic teaching through two dimensions: the "textual" divine religious imperative and the "contextual" public benefit consciousness for society. Here, the prohibition of *riba* should not be understood as a merely procedural compliance; the profound substantive objective in the prohibition should also be considered. It seems that the *fatwa* authorities have come to be concerned for this thoughtfulness in two dimensions as their basic reasoning in the procedure of extracting legal rules from Islamic law (*istinbath* process). For instance, Majelis Tarjih, Muhammadiyah has focused its legal argumentation on the "cause" (*illat*) of the prohibition of *riba* as the occurrence of "exploitation" leading to social injustice and mercilessness in economic transactions. On the other hand, Lajnah Bahsul Masa'il, NU tends to take a stand in accommodating and recognizing the various arguments of the controversy over the prohibition of bank interest. Meanwhile, MUI has emphasized the argument of the *illat*, insisting that the current practice of bank interest is considered as *riba*, because the cause is the incidence of "addition" (*ziyadah*) which is charged to the financial credit (loans). MUI is still in a conservative position in suggesting that the bank interest in modern financial transactions can be categorized as "usury of delay" (*riba al-nasi'ah*).

4. The genesis and development of Islamic banking in Indonesia

Islamic monetary economics and its initiatives to establish Islamic financial institutions, in particular, Islamic banks in the Muslim world, were developed in the 1970s. An important event perceived to be the trigger for this momentum was the first Islamic Economic Conference in Mecca, Saudi Arabia, in 1970 (Sardar, 1988; Haneef and Furqani, 2009; Wibisono, 2009). The conference was an essential starting point for the emergence of various strategic initiatives that can be labelled as "Islamic economy projects" in various Muslim countries (Choiruzzad, 2012). From the perspective of the construction of social institutions, what constituted an Islamic economy project was called the spirit of Islamization in the economy by Muslim scholars in the 1980s.[1]

The idea of Islamization of economics initially manifested in the form of various publishing activities, conference centres, and the establishment of Islamic economics at different universities in the Islamic world (Sardar, 1988). These strategic efforts did not end at the stage of conceptual ideas; the movement of the Islamization of economics also implemented real projects in the form of experiments to establish financial institutions based on the principles of Islam, with distinctive characteristics that operate without interest and that encourage the practice of profit-and-loss sharing in banking operations.

According to Iqbal and Mirakhor (2007), this effort in establishing interest-free financial institutions by the pioneers of the Islamization of economy project in the Muslim world was driven by Muslim scholars who were conscious of the prohibition of *riba*. They also recognized that the credit system practised by the conventional banks in the spirit of capitalism might have had an adverse impact on the national economy. In this sense, Lewis and Algoud (2001) conclude that the main objectives of establishing the Islamic bank in a Muslim society are: (1) to eliminate interest in the banking business; (2) to create a fair redistribution of wealth; and (3) to achieve economic development goals.

The initiative to establish Islamic banks began in 1963, in Mit Ghamr, Egypt. It was intended as a pilot project for a rural savings bank. In the 1970s, following the establishment of the Islamic Development Bank in 1975, a number of Islamic financial institutions began flourishing in the Muslim world; among others were the Dubai Islamic Bank (1975), Faisal Islamic Bank in Egypt and Sudan (1977), and Kuwait Finance House (1977). In the Southeast Asia region, the Malaysian government had set up the Pilgrimage Fund Board in 1969, followed by Bank Islam Malaysia Berhad in 1983 (Ascarya and Yumanita, 2008; Wibisono, 2009; Darsono et al., 2017).

During this last decade, the Islamic financial industry was acknowledged as one of the fastest growing segments in the global financial system (IFSB, 2015; FSA, 2015). In 2018, the global Islamic finance industry recorded its total asset amount at USD 2.19 trillion (IFSB, 2019). This phenomenon of the global

Islamic finance growth not only occurred in the Muslim-majority countries, but also in western countries with non-Muslim populations as the majority. For example, the total assets of the Islamic banking and finance industry in Europe, North America, and Australia were worth USD 42.7 billion in 2010, a double growth from USD 21.4 billion in 2007 (Caple and DiVanna, 2010).

Even with the negative image of Islam in numerous western hemisphere countries, as a direct impact of the 9/11 tragedy in 2011, the Islamic banking and finance industry continues to grow in the West as an alternative to the conventional financial system (Henry and Wilson, 2004; Choiruzzad, 2012). For instance, London has been promoted by the UK government as an emerging global hub for the Islamic finance industry (Ainley et al., 2007). In 2010, the Financial Services and Markets Act 2000 Order 2010 was introduced by the UK Treasury to support Islamic finance and the issuance of corporate *sukuk* (Islamic bonds) within the UK, and the UK government launched an Islamic Finance Task Force with the aim of securing London's status as the western hub for the Islamic finance market in 2012.

The genesis of a Muslim middle class with increasing affluence was coupled with its rising awareness towards applying Islamic values in various aspects of its lives, leading to a preference for using non-interest-based banking systems and demands for a *halal* industry, including Muslim-friendly food and fashion. No less important is the need for diversifying investment of petrodollars in the western countries as a strategic move in response to the changing oil and gas industries in the global financial system.

In the last four decades, we have witnessed Islamic banks becoming a driving force in leading the Islamization economy project in Muslim countries and becoming a significant issue in the current global financial system. In 2018, the global Islamic banking industry was estimated at USD 1.57 trillion with its share in total worth of the global Islamic financial services industry at about 71.7 per cent (IFSB, 2019).

In Indonesia, efforts in pioneering the establishment of Islamic financial institutions were initiated by the inception of several microfinance institutions and cooperatives which operated on Islamic principles. These grassroots institutions mainly provided Islamic microfinancing dedicated to alleviating poverty and developing small and medium enterprises in the 1980s. The inception of Baitut Maal wat-Tamwil (BMT), Ridho Gusti at Masjid Salman, Institut Teknologi Bandung in Bandung, and BMT Insan Kamil in Jakarta are some examples of such institutions (Ascarya and Yumanita, 2008; Darsono et al., 2017).

In fact, the idea of establishing a fully-fledged Islamic bank in accordance with banking regulations in Indonesia can be traced to the event of an MUI symposium on 18–20 August 1990, with the theme of "The problems of prohibition of interest and banking". The symposium highlighted the basic ideas of Muslim scholars on the issues of Islamic economy and banking, which were later presented at the Fourth Annual Congress of MUI on 22–25 August 1990.

This congress resulted in recommendations for preparing a blueprint for establishing the first Islamic commercial bank in Indonesia. Consequently, the establishment of the first Islamic commercial bank in Indonesia was driven jointly by MUI, the Ikatan Cendekiawan Muslim Indonesia (ICMI, Association of Indonesian Muslim Intellectuals), Muslim businesspeople, and the government of Indonesia. Then, in 1991, began the historical development of modern Islamic banking in Indonesia with the inception of the first Islamic bank, namely PT Bank Muamalat Indonesia (BMI). BMI began operating officially in May 1992 after the enactment of the Banking Act No. 7 Year 1992 and Government Regulation (Peraturan Pemerintah/PP) No. 72 of 1992 on Profit and Loss Banking System, which provided a breakthrough opportunity in establishing the first Islamic bank in Indonesia with a profit-and-loss banking system (Ascarya and Yumanita 2008, Darsono et al., 2017).

Islamic finance and banking institutions promote an economic model which is based on the mode of risk and profit sharing (and loss bearing) under *Shari'ah*-based *mudaraba* (trust-based contract) and *musharaka* (equity-like partnership-based) contracts. Islamic banking and financial institutions also offer their services through *Shari'ah*-compliant trading-based transactions – seeking profits on sales – in the form of *murabaha* (mark-up), *bai-muajjal* (variant of *murabaha*), *bai-salam* (forward sale contract), and *ijara* (leasing) contracts, and so on.

Muslim depositors and investors have to comply with the *Shari'ah* principle of prohibition of *riba*. According to *Shari'ah* opinion (*fatwa*), if they receive a return or yield from interest-based banks, they would have to have it "purified" by separating it from their income, and letting the *riba* earning go to charity or *zakat* institutions (Bakar, 2008). This structure may lose the Muslim who is committed to obeying the *Shari'ah* principles, along with the incentive to place their deposit in interest-based banks, possibly resulting in financial disintermediation in society. We will discuss this issue further in Chapter 4.

5. Socio-political context of Islamic banking in Indonesia

It is not possible to observe the development of Islamic banks in Indonesia separately from relational patterns between the state and Islam. It is interesting to see ebb and flow in the dynamics between the government as the holder of authority within a nation state, and the Islamic *ummah* as an element of the civil society with inherent basic rights to actualize its religious identity as well as the economic democratization which it aspires to (Choiruzzad, 2012; Choiruzzad and Nugroho, 2013; Choiruzzad, 2013).

Throughout the New Order period (1966–1998) under Suharto's rule, the state did not always have positive responses towards the interests of Muslims in Indonesia. Indeed, there was a tendency for the state to act repressively against Islamic political groups considered detrimental to the political status quo dominated by military elites and secular stakeholders of the bureaucracy. This was reflected at least through the political antagonism between Islamic groups represented by Islamic scholars and political parties with military elites, and a group of economic policy-makers known as the "Berkeley Mafia" – prominent

Indonesian economists who obtained their degrees from the University of California, Berkeley, in the United States (Baswir, 2006).

There was a change of direction in Indonesia's political pendulum towards the end of Suharto's rule from the late 1980s to the late 1990s (Lindsey, 2012; Choiruzzad and Nugroho, 2013; Choiruzzad, 2013). Suharto's political conduct and policy embraced Islamic-oriented groups, in this case represented by scholars like, among others, the late Prof. Dr Nurcholis Madjid and Prof. Dr B.J. Habibie (Indonesia's former third president) through the ICMI (Latif, 2005). This shift of Suharto's political orientation was actually owed to a clash of interest between Suharto loyalists backed by his children, who just went into the business world, and the established military elites and Indonesian Chinese businesspeople.

This friction forced Suharto to look for another group of backers other than the old (incumbent) elites to maintain his position and political power. The Islamic groups were chosen because Suharto saw in them a potential in the coming political battle under the transforming Indonesian political constellation, due to their resilience under his regime's previously repressive stance. On the other side, we could observe that economic and social development as the result of structural transformation under the New Order government had unwittingly created a new batch of Muslim middle class that had been marginalized at the start of the regime, but that was characterized by its commitment towards Islamic principles (Booth, 1998; Hill, 2000; Basri, 2002). For instance, high economic growth and a stable political situation opened up broad employment opportunities in the business sector, along with the availability of wider chances to get a higher education at leading national and international universities.

Suharto's political attitude then became very accommodating towards the political Islamic groups. Under this context, we saw Suharto soften towards and even support the Islamization of economy movement, which later paved the way for Indonesia's first experiment with Islamic banks in 1992. It is worth noting that some relevant initiatives were sponsored by Suharto's children and cronies, *inter alia* Humpus Group owner Tommy Suharto and Nusamba Group owner Bob Hasan, who were competing for reputation and business against a group of Indonesian Chinese who started to part way with Suharto's policy.

It is interesting to look at the socio-political context of the development of Islamic banks in Indonesia from Hefner's (2008) viewpoint, which concludes that the dynamics of Islamic banking development in many Muslim countries have a similar pattern, in which the proponents of Islamic finance and banking needed to go through a process of coalition building with three main elements of the society: (1) Islamic scholars (*ulama*); (2) Muslim capital owners; and (3) "prominent actors within the state" who see political interest in it.

In the Indonesian context, this process also went through at least three phases. First was the friction that happened between Suharto and some military elites and Indonesian Chinese businesspeople who started to oppose his political and economic policies, a development which had started to unfold since the late 1980s. In the second phase, approximately from 1990 to 1998, Suharto shifted his political stance, from being authoritarian and not friendly to Muslims, to being authoritarian but friendly to them. This showed that initializing the Islamization of economy through the founding of the first Islamic bank was part of Suharto's bid to win political support from a new source: the political Islam. The third phase occurred during the fall of Suharto's New Order regime in 1998, which went through an economic reform and democratization era, and which entailed economic democratization, benefitting, among others, Islamic groups and allowing a more open market for Islamic banking.

This gave the main players of the banking and financial market, the capital owners, the incentive to take the opportunity in the up-and-coming Islamic banks. In this regard, we also saw that policy-makers in Bank Indonesia (the central bank), the Ministry of Finance, and the Financial Services Authority become more accommodating and supportive towards the development of Islamic banks in Indonesia. Such an accommodating stance was reflected in prominent banks, both state owned and private, facilitating the establishment of some Islamic banks as their subsidiaries.

Another important thing to be emphasized is that, although the development of Islamic banking in Indonesia is admittedly a bottom-up – in other words, not centralized – process initiated by civil society elements like the ICMI and MUI, this does not mean that the establishment of Islamic banks was purely due to the force of demand of previously excluded Indonesian Muslims as potential customers. Indeed, we could also see the development as Indonesia's Muslim *ummah*'s endeavour to actualize or project its religious identity into its economic life. It is worth noting here that, although the early initiative for establishing Indonesian Islamic banks was bottom-up and ad hoc, the active participation of the government and policy-makers would have been sought for coordinating a comprehensive Islamic financial system.

Moreover, the bid to establish Islamic banks can be seen as a way to facilitate Muslims who believed that they could not obtain returns from banking transactions which would otherwise involve *riba*. Furthermore, a *fatwa* which says that Muslims may not enjoy income from banking interest, and instead must channel them for *zakat* and charitable activities permitted under the *Shari'ah* to be used for community development, means that Muslims would have less economic incentive in placing their money in the interest-based system. Establishing Islamic banking would encourage previously hesitant Muslim potential customers to contribute to the system. This could, in turn, open up the way to increase the inclusion of the banking sector within Indonesian society, which is still admittedly low, and could contribute towards the society's economic welfare in general.

We also underline that the civil society movement to realize Islamic banking in Indonesia reflected a pressure-group activity by political Islam groups as part of their struggle for social justice in spirit and practice towards Muslims who were marginalized, politically and economically, throughout the New Order period.

In the context of a political economy that occurred in Indonesia, the development of Islamic banking has been perceived by the proponents of the Islamization of economics movement as an attempt to create social and economic justice for the people of Indonesia. It conforms to the view that the capitalistic and neoliberalist economics policy as taken by the New Order government has created worsening economic inequality and poverty problems (Damanhuri, 2010). In recognizing the large numbers in its Muslim population and the potential of plentiful natural resources, Indonesia is becoming a prospective centre for the development of Islamic banking and financial markets in the world.

The establishment and development of Islamic banking in Indonesia were expected to contribute to improving the low level of financial deepening and economic justice through wealth creation and wealth transfer in accordance with the *Shari'ah* principle (Bakar, 2008). However, it seems that the reality does not always go along with the expectation.

Note

1 Choiruzzad and Nugroho (2013, p. 258) define the "Islamization of economy" movement as "organized individuals, groups or movements which call and struggle for the Islamization of the economic system". This definition is congruent to Hefner (2008, p. 17) who defines Islamic economics as "a modern movement which asserts that traditions of law and organization provide a more just and equitable model for economic growth than do rival systems of western capitalism and socialism".

References

Abojeib, M., Mohamed Haneef, M.A., and Mohammed, M.O. (Eds) (2018) *Islamic Economics: Principle and Analysis.* Kuala Lumpur: International Shari'ah Research Academy for Islamic Finance (ISRA).

Achsien, I.H. (2000) *Investasi Syariah di Pasar Modal, Mengagas Konsep dan Praktek Manajemen Portofolio Syariah.* Jakarta: PT. Gramedia Pustaka Utama.

Ainley, M., Mashayekhi, A., Hicks, R., and Rayalia, A. (2007) *Islamic Finance in the UK: Regulation and Challenges.* London: The Financial Service Authority.

Antonio, M.S. (2010) *Bank Syariah dari Teori ke Praktik.* Jakarta: Gema Insani Press.

Ascarya and Yumanita, D. (2008) Comparing the efficiency of Islamic Banks in Malaysia and Indonesia, *Buletin Ekonomi, Moneter dan Perbankan, 11*(2), pp. 95–119.

Ayub, M. (2007) *Understanding Islamic Finance.* Chichester: Wiley and Sons.

Bakar, M.D. (2008) Riba and Islamic banking and finance, in M.D. Bakar and E.R.A.E. Ali (Eds) *Essential Readings in Islamic Finance.* Kuala Lumpur: CERT Publication, pp. 3–23.

Basri, F.H. (2002) *Perekonomian Indonesia, Tantangan dan Harapan bagi Kebangkitan Indonesia.* Jakarta: Penerbit Erlangga.

Baswir, R. (2006) *Mafia Berkeley dan Krisis Ekonomi Indonesia.* Yogyakarta: Pustaka Pelajar.

Booth, A. (1998) *The Indonesian Economy in the Nineteenth and Twentieth Centuries, A History of Missed Opportunities.* London: Macmillan/New York: St. Martin's Press.

Caple, B. and DiVanna, J. (2010) Top 500 Islamic financial institutions, *The Banker*, 24 November 2010. Retrieved from: www.thebanker.com/Markets/Islamic-Finance/Top-500-Islamic-Financial-Institutions2

Ceiro, A. (2004) The social construction of Shari'a: Bank interest, home purchase, and Islamic norms in the West, *Die Welt des Islams, 44*(3), pp. 351–375.

Chapra, M.U. (1992) *Islam and Economic Challenge.* Leicester: The Islamic Foundation.

Chapra, M.U. (2000) *The Future of Economics: An Islamic Perspective.* Leicester: The Islamic Foundation.

Choiruzzad, S.A.B. (2012) The Central Bank in the development of Islamic economy project in Indonesia: Role, motivations and moderating effect, *The Ritsumeikan Journal of International Studies*, *25*(2), pp. 437–460.

Choiruzzad, S.A.B. (2013) More gain, more pain: The development of Indonesia's Islamic economy movement (1980s–2012), *Indonesia*, *2013*(95), pp. 125–172. doi: https://doi.org/10.5728/indonesia.95.0125

Choiruzzad, S.A.B. and Nugroho, B.E. (2013) Indonesia's Islamic economy project and the Islamic scholars, *Procedia Environmental Science*, *17*(2013), pp. 957–966.

Damanhuri, D.S. (2010) *Ekonomi Politik dan Pembangunan.* Bogor, Indonesia: PT Penerbit IPB Press.

Darsono et al. (2017) *Perbankan Syariah di Indonesia, Kelembagaan dan Kebijakan serta Tantangan ke Depan.* Jakarta: Rajawali Pers.

Financial Services Authority (FSA). (2015) *Roadmap of Indonesian Islamic Banking 2015–2019 (Roadmap Perbankan Syariah Indonesia 2015–2019).* Jakarta: FSA, Republic of Indonesia.

Haneef, M.A. and Furqani, F. (2009) Contemporary Islamic economics: The missing dimension of genuine Islamization, *Thought on Economics 19*(4), pp. 29–48.

Hefner, R.W. (2008) Global trends in Islamic finance: Social legacies and institutional variations, *NBR Research Report, March*, pp. 21–30.

Henry, C.M. and Wilson, R. (Eds). (2004) *The Politics of Islamic Finance.* Edinburgh: Edinburgh University Press.

Hill, H. (2000) *The Indonesian Economy.* Cambridge: Cambridge University Press.

Iqbal, Z. and Mirakhor, A. (2007) *An Introduction to Islamic Finance, Theory and Practice.* Singapore: John and Wiley and Sons.

Islamic Financial Service Board (IFSB). (2015) *IFSB's Islamic Financial Services Industry (IFSI) Stability Report 2015.* Kuala Lumpur: IFSB.

Islamic Financial Service Board (IFSB). (2019). *IFSB's Islamic Financial Services Industry (IFSI) Stability Report 2019.* Kuala Lumpur: IFSB.

Ismal, R. (2013) *Islamic Banking in Indonesia: New Perspectives on Monetary and Financial Issues.* Singapore: John Wiley and Sons.

Laldin, M.A. (2007) *A Mini Guide to Shariah & Legal Maxims.* Kuala Lumpur: CERT Publication.

Latif, Y. (2005) *Inteligensia Muslim dan Kuasa, Geneologi Inteligensia Muslim Indonesia Abad-20.* Bandung: Penerbit Mizan.

Lee, M.P. and Detta, I.J. (2007) *Islamic Banking and Finance Law.* Selangor Darul Ihsan: Pearson Malaysia Sdn Bhd.

Lewis, M.K. and Algoud, L.M. (2001) *Islamic Banking.* Cheltenham, UK: Edward Elgar.

Lindsey, T. (2012). Between piety and prudence: State Syariah and the regulation of Islamic banking in Indonesia, *Sydney Law Review*, *34*(107), pp. 1–16.

Sardar, Z. (1988) *Islamic Futures: The Shape of Ideas to Come.* Kuala Lumpur: Pelanduk Publication.

Wibisono, Y. (2009) Politik ekonomi UU perbankan Syariah peluang dan tantangan regulasi industri perbankan Syariah, *Bisnis dan Birokrasi, Jurnal Ilmu Administrasi dan Organisasi*, *16*(2), pp. 105–115.

3 Recent development of Indonesia's Islamic banking

The economic realities

1. Introduction

In the past four decades, Islamic finance and banking have rapidly expanded with a vigorous performance in financial indicators (Iqbal and Mirakhor, 2007; ADB and IFSB, 2015; IFSB, 2015). This chapter reviews the phenomenon of the growth of Islamic finance on a global scale. Subsequently, it sheds light on the realities in the recent development of Indonesia's Islamic banking.

On the one hand, regulators and several scholars suggest that Indonesian Islamic banking has demonstrated a progressive growth performance over the last two decades (Ismal, 2011, 2014; FSA, 2015a–2019a; Sukmana and Kuswanto, 2015). This is reflected in a robust performance that includes a relatively sound financial ratio indicator as well as a relatively stable performance in terms of funding and financing activities. On the other hand, we should not overlook the phenomenon of the extraordinarily low level of Islamic financial deepening and the slow-paced growth of Indonesia's Islamic banking. It is noticeable that the market share of Indonesian Islamic banks has been stagnant at about 3 to 6 per cent of the total Indonesian banking industry during the period of 2009–2018. Moreover, in the first decade of the 2000s, and during the period from 2005 to 2018, a trend of slow-paced growth in Indonesia's Islamic banking was observed (BI, 2004a–2014a; FSA, 2015a–2019a).

In this chapter, we present a comparative analysis between Islamic banks and conventional banks in Indonesia to review the ratios of return on assets (ROA), operational costs to operational incomes (OCOI), and non-performing loans/non-performing financing (NPL/NPF), and the loan-to-deposit/financing-to-deposit ratios (LDR/FDR). In addition, we scrutinize the growth of the institutional and infrastructure development of Indonesian Islamic banks, especially after the enactment of Act No. 21 in 2008 concerning Islamic banking. We attempt to clarify the profit base – probably the weakest base as the economic reality for Indonesia's Islamic banks.

The rest of this chapter is organized as follows. Section 2 begins with a brief discussion of the global development of Islamic finance. Then, Section 3 critically reviews the recent development and performance of Indonesian Islamic banks in comparison with those of conventional banks. Section 4 summarizes the discussion.

2. A brief discussion of the global development of Islamic finance

According to the Islamic Financial Service Board's (IFSB) *Islamic Financial Services Industry (IFSI) Stability Report 2015*, global Islamic finance showed an impressive growth trajectory during the period from 2009 to 2013. The industry accounted for the total asset amount of USD 1.87 trillion at the first half 2014, and recorded a double-digit compound annual growth rate (CAGR) of 17 per cent between 2009 and 2013. Subsequently, the IFSB's *Islamic Financial Services Industry (IFSI) Stability Report 2019* showed a continuous improvement of the global Islamic financial industry during 2015–2018. Its total worth reached USD 2.19 trillion at the first half of 2018. However, it is worth noting that a slightly fluctuated and slower growth rate was recorded in the period of 2015–2018, ranging from 0.6 per cent to 8.5 per cent (0.7 per cent in 2015, 0.6 per cent in 2016, 8.5 per cent in 2017, 6.9 per cent in 2018).

It is obvious that the Islamic banking sector is the dominant segment of the global Islamic finance industry. Global Islamic banking assets (covering fully-fledged Islamic banks, subsidiaries, and *Shari'ah* windows) amounted to about USD 1.48 trillion and shared about 79 per cent of the global Islamic finance assets in mid-2014 (IFSB, 2015). In 2018, the Islamic banking sector had attained USD 1.57 trillion and contributed to approximately 71.7 per cent of the total assets of the global Islamic financial industry (IFSB, 2019). As for the rate of growth, the Islamic banking sector grew at a CAGR of 16.89 per cent between 2008 and 2013. In 2014, the growth rate stayed at around 15 per cent (IFSB, 2015). Recently, global Islamic banking growth has slowed down; during the period of 2015–2018, it ranged from -0.2 per cent to 4.29 per cent (1.38 per cent in 2015; -0.21 per cent in 2016; 4.29 per cent in 2017; 0.89 per cent in 2018).

According to the "systemic importance" or "global systemic bank" categorization being used by the IFSB, Islamic banking with systemic importance in a country is expected to achieve at least 15 per cent market share of the total banking assets, and a global systemic bank is expected to hold more than 5 per cent of the total global Islamic banking assets (IFSB, 2015). First, let us look at the latter benchmark. ADB and IFSB (2015) expected that Islamic finance based upon *Shari'ah* principles would bring a new addition to the banking spectrum, and that Islamic banks, as lenders, would share project risks with their clients as borrowers. In addition, the preference for the real-asset-underlaid transactions in the Islamic mode of financing may discourage clients to make speculative investments which periodically cause financial bubbles. Meanwhile, we should note the reality in which Islamic finance is still less than 1 per cent of the global financial assets.

In passing, it is worth noting that apart from Iran and Sudan where a *Shari'ah*-compliant banking system alone is allowed to operate, there exist only ten countries with a *Shari'ah*-compliant banking system operating within a dual banking system: Brunei Darussalam, Saudi Arabia, Kuwait, Malaysia, Qatar, the United

Table 3.1 Comparison of Islamic bank market share and Muslim population in selected Muslim countries

Countries	*Resident Muslim population (2010, in million)*	*Percentage in population (2010)*	*Percentage Islamic banks' market share (2018)*
Indonesia	204.8	88.1	5.9
Malaysia	17.13	61.4	26.5
Saudi Arabia	25.50	97.1	51.5
Bangladesh	148.61	90.4	20.1
Pakistan	178.1	96.4	12.9

Source: Pew Research Center (2011); IFSB (2019); FSA (2015–2019).

Arab Emirates (UAE), Bangladesh, Djibouti, Jordan, and Bahrain, as of mid-2018 (IFSB, 2019). Next, let us look at the former benchmark. Among these countries, Islamic banking in Brunei Darussalam achieved a share of 63.6 per cent of total banking assets, and Saudi Arabia had a share of 51.5 per cent. It was 40.6 per cent in Kuwait, 26.5 per cent in Malaysia, 25.2 per cent in Qatar, 20.6 per cent in UAE, 20.1 per cent in Bangladesh, 15.5 per cent in Jordan, and around 14 per cent in Bahrain.[1] Following the former benchmark, these countries are classified as belonging to the systemic importance category by the IFSB. In general, while Islamic financial deepening is observed at a considerable level in the Gulf Cooperation Council countries, a limited level is observed in Asian Muslim countries (IFSB, 2019).

Islamic banking in Indonesia has not yet reached the level required for entry into the systemic importance category. At the end of 2018, Islamic banking in Indonesia booked its total assets at IDR 477 trillion, with total deposits of IDR 372 trillion and total financing at IDR 320 trillion. The market share of Indonesia's Islamic banks stayed at no more than 6 per cent of the total Indonesian banking industry during the period from 2004 to 2018 (Ismal, 2014; Sukmana and Kuswanto, 2015; FSA, 2015a–2019a). This leaves us with a big puzzle: compared to the other Muslim countries, why is Indonesia's Islamic financial deepening at an extraordinarily low level, despite having the largest Muslim population (see Table 3.1)?

3. Critical review of recent development and performance of Indonesian Islamic banking

During the period from 2004 to 2013, the growth of Islamic banks attained a higher level in comparison to the growth of conventional banks. Nevertheless, we should note that since 2005, the growth of both assets and financing in Islamic banks has slowed down. Moreover, we witness that in the period of 2014–2018, the growth of Islamic banks in Indonesia stayed at a moderate level, which was mostly the same level as their conventional banking counterparts (see Figure 3.1).

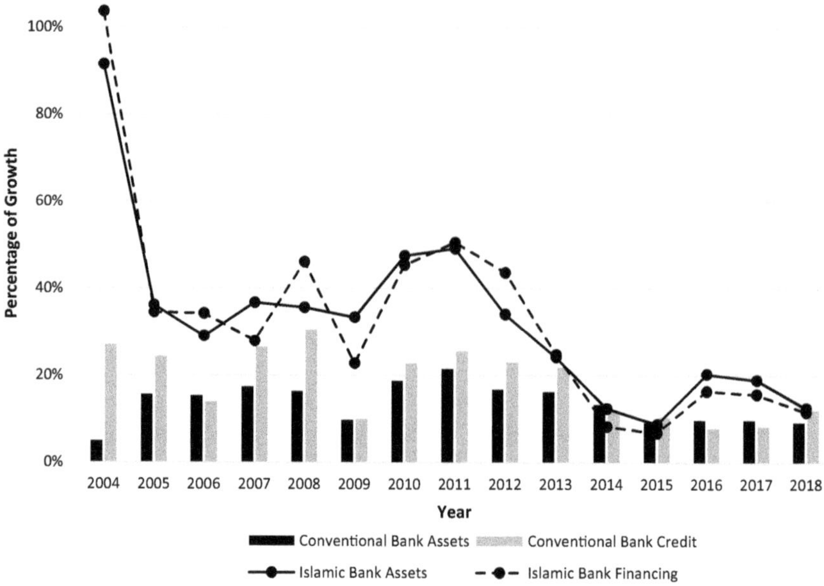

Figure 3.1 Comparison of Islamic and conventional bank growth .
Source: FSA (2015–2019, 2015a–2019a); constructed by the authors.

Table 3.2 shows the details of the growth of Islamic banking in Indonesia in terms of its total assets, total financing, total deposits, and market share during the period of 2003–2018.

This table reveals that the significant increase in the nominal terms of the Islamic bank assets did not automatically bring a significant increase in the market share (see Figure 3.2, which shows a comparison of total assets of Islamic banks and conventional banks during the period 2003 to 2018). Table 3.2 also clarifies the trend of slow-paced growth. In the year 2018, the growth of assets, financing, and deposits of Islamic banks fell to 12.5 per cent, 11.6 per cent, and 11.1 per cent, respectively. Even over a longer period, we observe that the growth of Islamic banks in Indonesia has been following a declining trend (see also Figure 3.1).

With regard to the growth performance of the market share of Islamic banks, Bank Indonesia (BI) (the former regulatory and supervisory authority for Indonesia's banking industry before the establishment of the Indonesian Financial Service Authority (FSA, Otoritas Jasa Keuangan) in accordance with Act No. 21 Year 2011 regarding FSA in 2011) had issued a number of policy documents and strategies to provide guidance for all stakeholders. These included: the *Blueprint of Islamic Banking Development in Indonesia*, Market Development Strategic Programme, Outlook of Islamic Banking, and the Islamic Banking Accelerated Programmes (BI, 2006) (we will discuss these strategic documents further in

Table 3.2 Indonesia's Islamic banking growth performance, 2003–2018

Year	*Market share*	*Total asset*	*Total financing*	*Total deposit*	*Growth*		
					Asset	*Financing*	*Deposit*
2003	0.7%	7,944	5,561	5,759	96.4%	69.7%	97.4%
2004	1.2%	15,210	11,324	11,718	91.5%	103.6%	103.5%
2005	1.4%	20,880	15,232	15,581	37.3%	34.5%	33.0%
2006	1.6%	26,722	20,445	20,672	28.0%	34.2%	32.7%
2007	1.7%	33,016	26,149	25,473	23.6%	27.9%	23.2%
2008	2.1%	49,555	38,199	36,852	50.1%	46.1%	44.7%
2009	2.6%	66,090	46,886	52,271	33.4%	22.7%	41.8%
2010	3.2%	97,519	68,181	76,036	47.6%	45.4%	45.5%
2011	3.6%	132,462	102,655	115,415	35.8%	50.6%	51.8%
2012	4.6%	195,018	147,505	147,512	47.2%	43.7%	27.8%
2013	4.9%	242,276	184,122	183,534	24.2%	24.8%	24.4%
2014	4.9%	272,343	199,330	217,858	12.4%	8.3%	18.7%
2015	4.8%	296,262	212,996	231,176	8.8%	6.9%	6.1%
2016	5.3%	356,504	248,007	279,335	20.3%	16.4%	20.8%
2017	5.7%	424,181	286,849	334,719	19.0%	15.7%	19.8%
2018	5.9%	477,327	320,193	371,828	12.5%	11.6%	11.1%

Source: FSA (2015–2019, 2015a–2019a); Sukmana and Kuswanto (2015).

Chapter 5). One of the most important among these are the Islamic Banking Accelerated Programmes, basically aimed at achieving the quantitative target of increasing the market share of Islamic banks to 5.25 per cent by the end of 2008. In fact, it was in 2016 when this target was finally achieved.

It is worth noting that the Islamic banks' achievement of 5–6 per cent of market share in 2016–2018 did not only result from the "organic growth" of the Islamic banking business, but owed more to the strategic acquisition carried out by the Regional Development Bank (Bank Pembangunan Daerah) by converting its conventional banks owned by local governments into fully-fledged Islamic banks. These included: PT Bank Aceh Syariah (owned by the provincial government of Nanggroe Aceh Darussalam Province) according to the decree of FSA No. KEP-44/D.03/2016 dated 1 September 2016; and PT Bank NTB Syariah (owned by the provincial government of West Nusa Tenggara Province) according to the decree of FSA No. KEP-145/D.03/2018 dated 24 September 2018.

Act No. 7 of 1992 on Banking Article 29 states that BI has the right to stipulate the provision of a bank's health level, with regard to its capital, asset quality, earnings, liquidity, solvency, and other aspects related to the business of the regulated bank. Furthermore, BI issued a Director's Decree of BI No. 30/277/KEP/DIR dated 19 March 1998 that governs how to assess the health level of a bank. As for Islamic banks, BI Circular Letter No. 9/24/DPbS concerning the Rating System for Commercial Banks based on *Shari'ah* principles came into effect on 30 October 2007. The rating of commercial banks based on *Shari'ah* principles considers the CAMELS indicators (capital adequacy, asset quality,

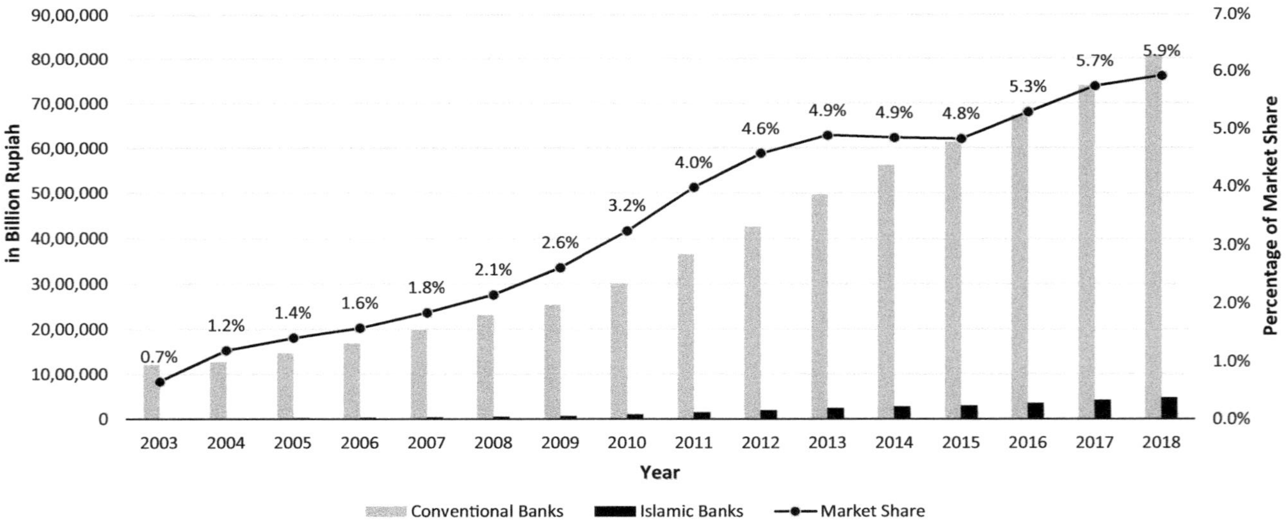

Figure 3.2 Comparison of total assets of Indonesia's conventional and Islamic banks, and Islamic banks' market share performance in period 2003–2018.

Source: BI (2004–2014, 2004a–2014a) FSA (2015–2019, 2015a–2019a); constructed by the authors.

management quality, earnings, and liquidity capability) by measuring the effect of financial and management (non-financial) factors on a bank's performance.

Here, in accordance with BI Circular Letter No. 9/24/DPbS concerning the Rating System for Commercial Banks based on *Shari'ah* principles, we look at ROA, OCOI, NPF, FDR, and net profit margin (NPM). Table 3.3 presents these financial performance indicators of Islamic and conventional banks during the period 2005–2018. This table suggests that the overall performance of Indonesia's Islamic banks has been, as a whole, lower than that of conventional banks.

During the period from 2005 to 2018, ROA of the Islamic banks was lower than that of conventional banks. In fact, we see the gap in profitability between Islamic banks and conventional banks being widened. This indicates that the profit base of Islamic banks is not so strong as that of conventional banks. Looking at OCOI, conventional banks seem to have successfully managed to increase their efficiency (declining trend of OCOI). Recently, OCOI of Islamic banks was even higher than conventional banks. In general, this empirical study suggests that the operation of Islamic banks is not so efficient as that of conventional banks.

The recent level of NPF of Islamic banks was higher than that of NPL in conventional banks. We also note that while the ratio of NPL in conventional banks has been on a decreasing trend, the ratio of NPF in Islamic banks has stayed in a certain range during the period of 2005–2018. The LDR of conventional banks was on an increasing trend, while that of Islamic banks was volatile, but on a declining trend during the period from 2005 to 2018. This assumes that while conventional banks were improving their function as financial intermediaries, Islamic banks were not.

Finally, looking at net interest margin (NIM) for conventional banks, which measures the ratio of interest spread generated by conventional banks to the total productive assets owned by the banks, and NPM for Islamic banks, which describes the ratio of profit-and-loss margin of Islamic banks' profit-sharing business to the total productive assets owned by them, we see that conventional banks enjoyed higher NIM than the NPM of Islamic banks during this period.

We should note that according to BI Regulation No. 14/26/PBI/2012 (BI, 2012), the Indonesian regulator classifies commercial banks based on their core capital and stipulates the permitted activities for each category, namely *Bank Umum berdasarkan Kegiatan Usaha* (BUKU/commercial bank-based business activities). For this purpose, the regulation restricts the scope of commercial banks' business activities, such as the maximum credit/financing limit, and boundaries in expanding new offices, based on the amount of core capital maintained by the regulated banks. A brief summary of the detailed BUKU classification for commercial banks according to BI Regulation No. 14/26/PBI/2012 (BI, 2012) is shown in Table 3.4.

According to *the Indonesian Islamic Banking Statistics December 2018* (FSA, 2015a–2019a), as of 31 December 2018, most of the fully-fledged Islamic banks were classified in the BUKU 1 and 2 categories; only one Islamic bank was classified as BUKU 3. In general, Indonesia's Islamic banks operate on thin capital bases. Scholars and the regulatory authorities are concerned about the size

Table 3.3 Indonesian banking financial performance indicators, 2005–2018

Financial indicators	*2005*	*2006*	*2007*	*2008*	*2009*	*2010*	*2011*	*2012*	*2013*	*2014*	*2015*	*2016*	*2017*	*2018*
Return on assets (ROA)														
Conventional bank	2.6	2.6	2.8	2.3	2.6	2.9	3.0	3.1	3.1	2.9	2.3	2.2	2.5	2.6
Islamic bank	1.4	1.6	2.1	1.4	1.5	1.6	1.6	1.9	1.6	0.4	0.8	0.9	1.2	1.6
Operating cost to operating income (OCOI)														
Conventional bank	89.5	87.0	84.1	88.6	86.6	86.1	85.4	74.1	74.1	76.3	81.5	82.2	78.6	77.9
Islamic bank	78.9	76.8	76.5	81.8	84.4	82.4	81.7	76.4	82.2	94.2	94.4	93.6	89.6	85.5
Non-performing loan/ financing (NPL/NPF)														
Conventional bank	7.6	6.1	4.1	3.2	3.3	2.6	2.2	1.9	1.8	2.2	2.5	2.9	2.6	2.4
Islamic bank	2.8	4.8	4.1	4.0	4.0	3.0	2.5	2.3	2.6	4.3	4.3	4.2	3.9	2.9
Loan/financing-to-deposit ratio (LDR/FDR)														
Conventional bank	59.7	61.6	66.3	74.6	72.9	75.2	78.8	83.6	89.7	89.4	92.1	90.7	90.0	94.8
Islamic bank	97.8	98.9	99.8	103.7	89.7	87.6	91.4	120.7	95.9	86.7	92.1	88.8	85.3	86.1
Net interest/profit margin (NIM/NPM)														
Conventional bank	5.6	5.8	5.7	5.7	5.6	5.7	5.9	5.5	4.9	4.2	5.4	5.6	5.3	5.1
Islamic bank	NA	NA	NA	NA	NA	1.8	1.2	2.0	1.8	2.9	0.9	1.0	1.3	1.7

Source: BI (2004–2014, 2004a–2014a) FSA (2015–2019, 2015a–2019a).

Table 3.4 Classification of the commercial banks in Indonesia by type of commercial bank-based business activities (BUKU)

BUKU	*Core capital amount*	*Products and activities coverage*
1	Less than Rp 1 trillion	1. Basic Rupiah intermediary functions for deposit and financing, trade finance, limited agency/cooperation, limited electronic banking and payment systems, temporary capital participation for credit-based or other services, and limited foreign exchange 2. Branches only within Indonesia 3. No capital participation in other financial institutions 4. Must distribute 55% of total credit/financing to productive business
2	Rp 1 – 5 trillion	1. Same business activities as BUKU 1, but with higher transaction value 2. Branches only within Indonesia 3. Capital participation in other Indonesian financial institutions, up to 15% of capital 4. Must distribute 60% of total credit/financing to productive business
3	Rp 5 – 30 trillion	1. All types of business activities, in Rupiah and foreign currency 2. Branches and representative offices in Indonesia and Asia region 3. Capital participation in Indonesian and other Asian financial institutions, up to 25% of capital 4. Must distribute 65% of total credit/financing to productive business
4	At least Rp30 trillion	1. All types of business activities, in Rupiah and foreign currency 2. Worldwide branches and representative offices 3. Worldwide capital participation in other financial institutions, up to 35% of capital 4. Must distribute 70% of total credit/financing to productive business
*	Other regulations	– Business activity conducted by the Islamic business division (UUS) refers to BUKU classification of its conventional bank parent company. – Minimum capital participation for the conventional bank in its Islamic bank subsidiary is 5%. In this case, for the conventional bank categorized in BUKU 2 which, as the holding company for the Islamic bank, has maximum capital participation of 20%, whereas for the conventional bank categorized in BUKU 3 it is 30%.

Source: Bank Indonesia (2012). This summary of BI Regulation No. 14/26/PBI/2012 explanation is cited from Akset Law Firm's regulation news (http://aksetlaw.com/news-event/newsflash/new-bank-indonesia-regulation-on-multiple-licensing-policy/)

of equity capital as a buffer against unexpected loss (Bappenas, 2016). Table 3.5 shows a relatively lower level of capital adequacy ratio for Islamic banks than for conventional banks. We presume that thin capital bases in Indonesian Islamic banks make it difficult for them to compete with conventional banks, resulting in low profitability, inefficient operations, and a very conservative credit policy. Fewer opportunities for profit seeking may, in turn, lose them the opportunity to increase their capital bases. Perhaps, Indonesia's Islamic banks have fallen into a vicious circle.

To analyse the reasons behind the low profitability generally observed in Indonesia's Islamic banks, we look at the funding structure and the asset portfolios held by both Islamic and conventional banks.

First, as for the funding structure, on the whole there was no specific difference in the funding composition as "depository corporations" between Islamic banks and commercial banks in Indonesia, except that Islamic banks tend to rely more on time deposits than do conventional banks. For instance, 62 per cent in the funding portfolio of Islamic banks were time deposits as at the end of December 2014, and these accounted for 57 per cent as at the end of December 2018; while conventional banks reported 47 per cent and 44 per cent, respectively (see Figure 3.3). Table 3.6 shows the deposit rates offered or indicated by conventional and Islamic banks. It appears that both offered or indicated almost the same rates for the same type of deposit account, although the rates per se fluctuated during the investigated period. Presumably, owing to the extent to which Islamic banks tend to rely more on time deposits where the funding cost is high, their overall cost of funds is likely to be higher than that of conventional banks (see Table 3.6).

Second, we recall that not less than 94 per cent of the total financing (as of the end of 2018) is mediated by conventional banks in Indonesia. The presence of Islamic banks is marginal. As for the asset portfolio in conventional banks, the largest portfolio consists of short-term working capital, followed by consumer financing, and investment credit as the smallest. As for the credit portfolio in Islamic banks, the largest portfolio is made up of consumer financing upon *murabaha* contracts[2] (about 43 per cent in the portfolio as at the end of 2018; see Figure 3.4), followed by working capital credit, with the smallest made up of investment credit. The dominant credit portfolio of consumer financing in Islamic banking was noticeably continuous in the period of 2014–2018.

While Islamic banks' conservative credit policy made them focus on asset-based consumer financing in the automotive industry (automobiles/motorcycles), they were exposed to more severe competition with conventional banks. This was because there was no differentiation between the financing products for automobiles/motorcycles offered by them. Higher cost of funds in Islamic banks may have squeezed their profit margin because it is extremely difficult to simply apply "mark-up" pricing to compete with conventional banks in this segment.

Table 3.7 shows the offered rates for each type of financing provided by conventional and Islamic banks. We observe that Islamic banks offer higher rates in the type of working capital and investment financing than conventional banks,

Table 3.5 Comparison of the capital adequacy ratio (CAR) between conventional and Islamic banks in Indonesia for the period 2005–2018

Banks	*2005*	*2006*	*2007*	*2008*	*2009*	*2010*	*2011*	*2012*	*2013*	*2014*	*2015*	*2016*	*2017*	*2018*
Conventional bank – CAR	19.3	21.3	19.3	16.8	17.4	17.2	16.1	17.4	18.1	19.6	21.4	22.9	23.2	23.0
Islamic bank – CAR	12.4	13.7	10.7	12.8	10.8	16.8	15.4	14.1	14.4	15.7	15.0	16.6	17.9	20.4

Source: BI (2004–2014, 2004a–2014a) FSA (2015–2019, 2015a–2019a).

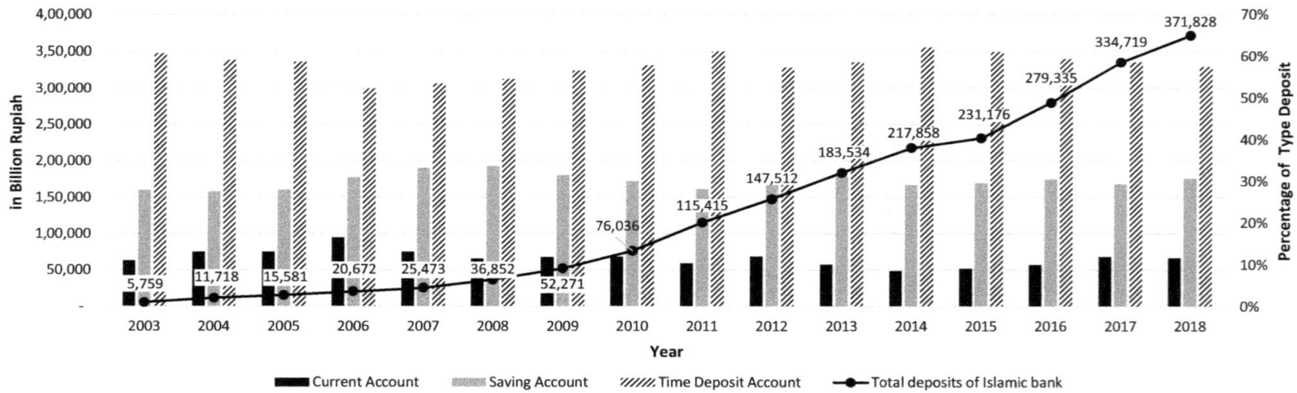

Figure 3.3 Total deposits and percentage composition of type of deposit: Indonesia's Islamic banks in the period 2003–2018.
Source: BI (2004–2014, 2004a–2014a) FSA (2015–2019, 2015a–2019a); constructed by the authors.

Table 3.6 Comparison of the rates for deposit funds collected by Indonesia's conventional and Islamic banks for the period 2008–2018

Type of deposit	*2008*	*2009*	*2010*	*2011*	*2012*	*2013*	*2014*	*2015*	*2016*	*2017*	*2018*
Savings account:											
Conventional banks – savings account rate	3.1	2.8	2.9	2.4	1.9	2.0	2.0	2.0	1.7	1.6	1.3
Islamic banks – savings account rate	3.6	2.8	3.1	3.2	2.4	5.7	3.6	3.6	2.4	2.4	2.1
Current account:											
Conventional banks – current account rate	2.9	2.4	2.2	2.4	2.1	2.1	2.3	2.2	2.2	2.2	2.2
Islamic banks – current account rate	1.2	1.0	1.3	2.2	1.0	0.7	0.7	1.2	1.6	1.5	2.1
Time deposit:											
Conventional banks – time deposit rate	10.7	6.8	6.6	6.4	5.6	7.7	8.6	7.6	6.5	5.7	6.9
Islamic banks – time deposit rate	8.6	7.5	7.0	7.5	6.3	5.1	8.4	7.5	6.3	5.9	6.0

Source: BI (2004–2014, 2004a–2014a) FSA (2015–2019, 2015a–2019a).

while interestingly, Islamic banks offer lower rates in the type of consumption (consumer) financing. Perhaps, less bargaining power for marketing and outreach in the limited office network may force Islamic banks to discount their offered rate to keep a competitive edge.

As at the end of 2018, Indonesia's Islamic banking industry had recorded 14 fully-fledged Islamic banks (*Bank Umum Syariah*) and 20 Islamic business units *(Unit Usaha Syariah*/UUS), and had reached a total of 1,875 branch offices throughout Indonesia (FSA, 2015a–2019a) (see Table 3.8). At the same time, conventional banks had expanded their total office network to 31,618 offices. Considering the Islamic banks' market share of not more than 6 per cent, we may say that the office-branch network of Islamic banks is a bit too large to operate efficiently. Also, we may say that the smaller number of Islamic banks' office branches (approximately only around 6 per cent of the network of conventional banks) may cost them their marketing and bargaining power from existing and potential customers. In passing, we should also note that the pace of expanding the office-branch network by Islamic banks has slowed down since 2013.

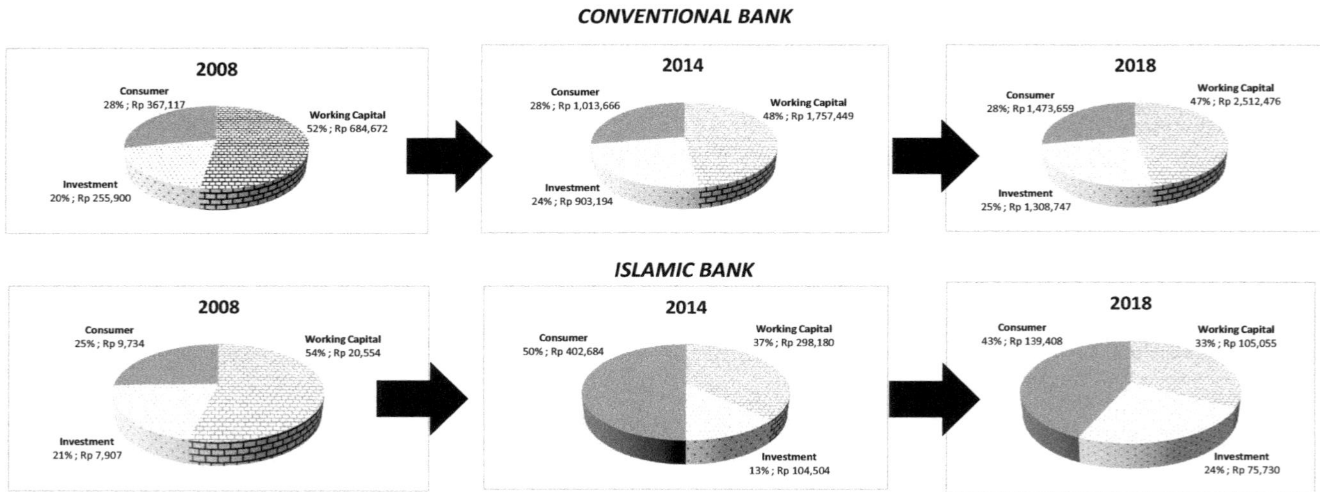

Figure 3.4 Comparison of composition of conventional and Islamic banks' credit/financing in 2008, 2014, and 2018.

Source: BI (2004–2014, 2004a–2014a) FSA (2015–2019, 2015a–2019a); constructed by authors.

Table 3.7 Comparison of rates for types of financing conducted by Indonesia's conventional and Islamic banks for the period 2008–2014

Type of financing	*2008*	*2009*	*2010*	*2011*	*2012*	*2013*	*2014*	*2015*	*2016*	*2017*	*2018*
Working capital:											
Conventional bank –Working capital rate	14.6	13.3	12.4	12.0	11.5	12.1	12.8	12.5	11.4	10.7	10.4
Islamic bank – working capital rate	19.3	17.2	17.0	15.7	14.6	13.7	18.3	15.3	15.4	13.7	12.8
Investment:											
Conventional bank –investment rate	14.0	12.6	11.9	11.7	11.3	11.8	12.4	12.1	11.2	10.6	10.4
Islamic bank – investment rate	18.0	14.2	14.8	14.7	14.4	13.3	15.4	13.1	12.1	11.1	10.4
Consumption:											
Conventional bank – consumption rate	15.8	15.8	13.8	13.4	13.6	13.1	13.6	13.9	13.6	12.7	11.7
Islamic bank – consumption rate	14.3	11.4	10.5	10.0	10.7	11.2	11.9	12.6	11.6	11.2	10.6

Source: BI (2004–2014, 2004a–2014a) FSA (2015–2019, 2015a–2019a).

Table 3.8 Numbers of Islamic banks, Islamic business units, and office networks in Indonesia

	2003	*2004*	*2005*	*2006*	*2007*	*2008*	*2009*	*2010*	*2011*	*2012*	*2013*	*2014*	*2015*	*2016*	*2017*	*2018*
Islamic banks: numbers	2	3	3	3	3	5	6	11	11	11	11	12	12	13	13	14
Islamic business units: numbers	8	16	19	20	25	27	25	23	24	24	23	22	22	21	21	20
Total offices: branch network	265	355	458	531	597	822	998	1,477	1,737	2,262	2,588	2,471	1,990	1,869	1,825	1,875

Source: BI (2004–2014, 2004a–2014a) FSA (2015–2019, 2015a–2019a).

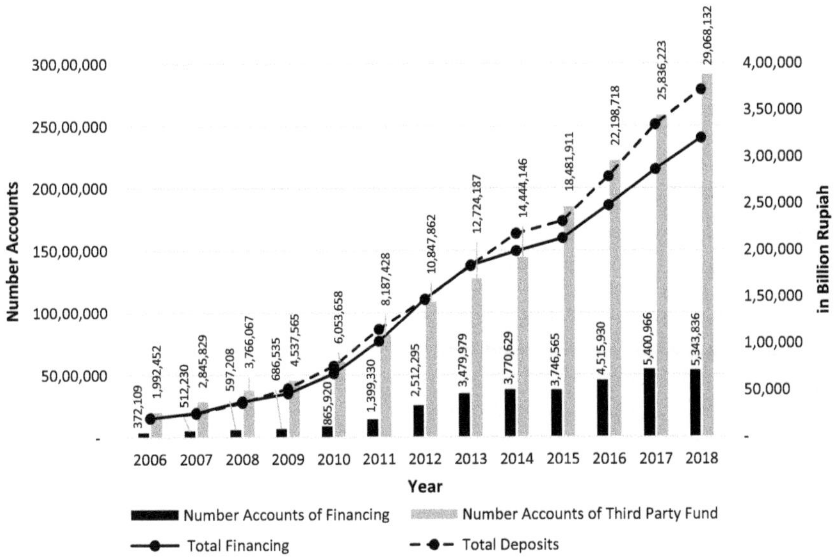

Figure 3.5 Development of accounts of financing, and of third-party funds, total financing, and total deposits in Indonesia's Islamic banks in the period 2006–2018.

Source: FSA (2015–2019, 2015a–2019a); constructed by the authors.

With regard to the development of the number of accounts of financing and third-party fund (deposits) in Indonesia's Islamic banking, Figure 3.5 shows that even though the number of accounts increased in the period of 2003–2018, the average nominal amount per account had not increased as much. As of 2018, we estimate the average nominal amount per account of financing was about IDR 60 million, while that of deposits was IDR 13 million. Presumably, Islamic banks have not yet obtained the economies of scale to compete with conventional banks.

4. Summary

In this chapter, we analysed the economic reality behind the low level – a share of not more than 6 per cent – of Islamic financial deepening in Indonesia. Our investigation clarified how Indonesia's Islamic banks suffered from lower profitability, lower efficiency, thinner capital bases, higher cost of funds, and a smaller office-branch network than what conventional banks had achieved. This structural problem may have undermined the profit base for Islamic banks and lost them their edge to compete with conventional banks.

In particular, although the main business strategy by most Indonesian Islamic banks is to penetrate into the "retail banking market" (Bappenas, 2016), they have not yet attained the economies of scale necessary for this penetration. Their low profitability or thin capital bases may have hampered their strategy of expanding their branch networks, while the limited outreach to serve their potential customers may have fixed their low profitability or thin capital bases. We assume that this dilemma may have interlocked with the slow-paced growth of Indonesia's Islamic banking industry since 2012.

Notes

1 IFSB had discretion to put Bahrain in the "systemic importance" Islamic banking industry category although it only held around 14 per cent of share (IFSB, 2019). IFSB decided to take into consideration other factors: (1) a jurisdiction (financial system regime) which was within one percentage point of the 15 per cent benchmark; and (2) that this country should be among the top ten jurisdictions of either the Islamic capital market sector or *Takaful* industry.

2 A *murabaha* financing contract is one of the finance products in the Islamic banking business which is categorized under *Shari'ah*-compliant asset-based financing modes. Basically, a *murabaha* financing agreement will offer asset-reselling transactions with a determined profit; for example, the Islamic bank will purchase a certain asset and will sell it to the bank customer on the basis of a cost-plus mark-up profit principle.

References

Asian Development Bank (ADB) and Islamic Financial Service Board (IFSB). (2015) *Islamic Finance for Asia: Development, Prospects, and Inclusive Growth.* Manila: ADB and IFSB.

Badan Perencanaan Pembangunan Nasional (Bappenas). (2016) *Masterplan Arsitektur Keuangan Syariah di Indonesia.* Jakarta: Bappenas.

Bank Indonesia (BI). (2004–2014) *Indonesian Banking Statistics December 2003–2013.* Jakarta: BI.

Bank Indonesia (BI). (2004a–2014a) *Indonesian Islamic Banking Statistics December 2003–2013.* Jakarta: BI.

Bank Indonesia (BI). (2006) *Blueprint of Islamic Banking Development in Indonesia.* Jakarta: BI.

Bank Indonesia (BI). (2012). Peraturan Bank Indonesia NOMOR 14/26/PBI/2012 Tentang Kegiatan Usaha dan Jaringan Kantor Berdasarkan Modal Inti Bank. Retrieved from: www.bi.go.id/id/peraturan/perbankan/Pages/pbi_142612.aspx

Financial Services Authority (FSA). (2015–2019) *Indonesian Banking Statistics December 2014–2018.* Jakarta: FSA, Republic of Indonesia.

Financial Services Authority (FSA). (2015a–2019a) *Indonesian Islamic Banking Statistics December 2014–2018.* Jakarta: FSA, Republic of Indonesia.

Iqbal, Z. and Mirakhor, A. (2007) *An Introduction to Islamic Finance, Theory and Practice.* Singapore: John and Wiley and Sons.

Islamic Financial Service Board (IFSB). (2015) *IFSB's Islamic Financial Services Industry (IFSI) Stability Report 2015.* Kuala Lumpur: IFSB.

Islamic Financial Service Board (IFSB). (2019) *Islamic Financial Services Industry (IFSI) Stability Report 2019.* Kuala Lumpur: IFSB.

Ismal, R. (2011) Islamic banking in Indonesia: Lessons learnt. Paper presented at *Multi-Year Expert Meeting on Services, Development and Trade: The Regulatory and Institutional Dimension*, Geneva, 6–8 April 2011.

Ismal, R. (2014) Indonesia, the resilience and prospects of Islamic banking, in S. Thiagaraja et al. (Eds) *The Islamic Finance Handbook, A Practitioner's Guide to the Global Market*, Singapore: John Wiley and Sons, pp. 155–173.

Pew Research Center. (2011) The future of the global Muslim population: Projections for 2010–2030. Retrieved from: http://assets.pewresearch.org/wpcontent/uploads/sites/11/2011/01/FutureGlobalMuslimPopulationWebPDF-Feb10.pdf

Sukmana, R., and Kuswanto, H. (2015) Assessment on the Islamic banking market share projection by Bank Indonesia and proposed methods, *Journal of Islamic Monetary Economics and Finance*, *1*(1), pp. 107–133.

4 Theoretical background and review of related literature

1. Introduction

In Chapter 3, we discussed how Indonesia's Islamic banks suffered from lower profitability, lower efficiency, thinner capital bases, higher cost of funds, and a smaller office-branch network than those achieved by conventional banks. Indonesian Islamic banks are apparently trapped in such a structural problem which may have undermined their profit base and lost them their competitive edge in the credit market and, in particular, in the consumer finance market.

It might be self-evident that the undermined profit base would hinder market penetration. However, we should consider fundamental questions, such as: How much should Islamic banks earn? What do they need to earn profits for? Should society protect their profit base? Is there any optimal level of profit margin for Islamic banks? To understand the structural problem faced by Indonesia's Islamic banks, we should attempt to answer these fundamental questions.

Several approaches have been attempted to explain the extraordinarily low development penetration and the recent trend of slow-paced growth of Islamic banking in Indonesia (Kasri and Kassim, 2009; Lindsey, 2012; Sari et al., 2016). In our view, this problem was caused by the regulators' (or society's) failure to create an appropriate "incentive" for Islamic banks to become prudent and *Shari'ah*-compliant fund providers. Apparently, the arguments in the existing literature do not sufficiently shed analytical light on the mechanism of creating "incentive" and "threat" in the credit risk monitoring by Indonesia's Islamic banks.

In this chapter, in order to develop our theoretical framework for analysis, we draw upon the traditions of New Institutional Economics (NIE), which are concerned about the mechanism or institutions of creating incentive and threat for economic players. In particular, we draw on the theoretical framework of "financial sector rent" (bank rent) to justify the creation of a "rent (surplus) opportunity" to be captured by banks as the incentive to make them become prudent fund providers (Hellmann et al., 1997; Khan, 2000; Suzuki, 2011; Suzuki and Uddin, 2014). In our view, the low level of Indonesia's Islamic banking deepening was caused by state or institutional failure, rather than any individual Islamic bank's failure. The regulators' failure to create adequate rent opportunities for Islamic banks was the root cause of Indonesia's Islamic banking slump.

This chapter develops our theoretical framework to understanding the low level of Islamic financial deepening in Indonesia. The rest of this chapter is organized as follows: Section 2 gives an overview of the role of the financial sector rent to be captured by banks as the incentive for facilitating more financial resources. The market failure under the imperfect information paradigm is reviewed, and the "financial restraint" framework, such as applying "credit rationing" as a solution for the market failure, is argued in this section. In Section 3, we review the Islamic bank rent hypothesis by Suzuki and Uddin (2014). We point out how the regulators' policy of encouraging a free and competitive credit market among conventional and Islamic banks would amount to be harsh on Indonesia's Islamic banking industry if the hypothesis is held. Section 4 provides our concluding comments.

2. Theory of financial sector rent (bank rent)

Intrinsically, the financial market is perceived to have a different character in comparison to the commodity market. First, we realize that the market mechanism is quite often inattentive to clear imbalances in the financial market. This condition is the impulse for special attention to be given to the smoothing of financial market functions (Stiglitz, 1994). Second, it is recognized that the transactions in the financial market between debtors and creditors obviously contain a substantial degree of information asymmetry and imperfection in the market mechanism (Aoki, 1994; Suzuki, 2011), which can lead to adverse selection (*ex-ante*), coordination (interim), and moral hazard (*ex-post*) problems in the financial market (Aoki, 1994).

This imperfect financial market paradigm has been highlighted in many studies. Among others, Stiglitz and Weiss (1981) initiated a critical analysis on this paradigm. They argue that market failure is unavoidable in a financial market embedded with a substantial degree of information asymmetry. Accordingly, it is impossible to clear imbalances using market mechanisms in the credit market. Subsequently, the imperfection of the credit market is considered the main obstacle to attaining an efficient financial resource allocation, particularly in developing economies with serious asymmetry of information among the players.

Since market mechanisms do not apply effectively in a financial market that is naturally imbalanced, we should install an alternative mechanism for creating appropriate "incentives" to the players in the financial industry (Stiglitz, 1994; Wanniarachchige, 2017). The banking industry is exposed to a multiple principal–agent structure, including the structure between the lender (bank) and the borrower (client firm), between the bank's shareholder (or stakeholder) and the bank manager, between the depositor and the bank, between the regulator and the regulated bank, and so on. This book is mainly concerned about bank shareholders (or stakeholders) as well as the regulatory "failure" to create and maintain adequate incentives for the bank (or the bank manager) to become a prudent fund provider.

A free and unfettered market would not provide a proper incentive for banks to have qualified management or to realize the optimum allocation of funds in the financial market. In other words, it is arguable that a bank should receive a sufficient "rent" in terms of "surplus" as an incentive for encouraging the best effort in running its business. The financial sector rent (bank rent) opportunity has been studied as an effective incentive for prudent screening and monitoring, which consequently improves a bank's "franchise value" (Hellmann et al., 1997; Khan, 2000; Suzuki and Adhikary, 2009; Suzuki, 2011; Wanniarachchige, 2017; Suzuki et al., 2017).

Rent is defined as excess income or, "more precisely, a person gets a rent if he or she earns an income higher than the minimum that the person would have accepted, the minimum being usually defined as the income in his or her next-best opportunity" (Khan, 2000, p. 21). The bank rent opportunity to be captured by banks is considered as the "monitoring" or "management" rent to give bank managers the incentives to maintain their franchise value necessary to keep the banks' long-term performance. The term franchise value is defined by Demsetz et al. (1996, p. 2) as "the present value of the future profits that a firm is expected to earn as a going concern". The franchise value is an important element as the cost of ensuring the bank's management will provide good management assurance (Hellmann et al., 1997; Suzuki, 2011, p. 24).

The credits in the financial market are intrinsically rationed due to asymmetric information problems. Stiglitz and Weiss (1981) argue that the banks cannot perfectly perform the *ex-ante* selection process to choose only the creditworthy borrowers, and cannot perfectly monitor the behaviour of borrowers in the *ex-post* stage after the disbursement of credit. Hellmann et al. (1997) expand this theory. Their financial restraint model justifies the governmental initiative, which would set up a "ceiling" in the deposit market to create the rent opportunities (the gap between the lending rate and the regulated deposit rate) to be captured by banks as the incentive for them to pay their efforts to facilitate more financial resources. Adequate rents would encourage banks to improve their expertise in monitoring and in the intermediary capacity of loans to borrowers, thus enhancing the efficiency of financial resource allocation (Suzuki and Adhikary, 2009). In theory, it is plausible that the total volume of funds intermediated through the formal financial sector would be larger under the financial restraint policy, compared to the case under the free and unfettered market.

Hellmann et al. (1997, pp. 171–174) analyse the rent opportunities as an important driver to ensure an adequate profit base for the bank. In addition, they point out that the financial sector rent as an incentive for credit monitoring brings a "rent effect" in terms of increasing the returns to financial intermediation, in which banks have strong incentives to increase their own deposit bases. With the assumption that the amount of savings depends on the availability of infrastructure for deposit collection (branch network and quality of service), the increased savings will also increase the supply of the loanable fund (Suzuki and Adhikary, 2009).

Let us go back to the issue of the low level of Islamic banking penetration in Indonesia. In Chapter 3, we saw that Indonesian Islamic banks have been trapped into such a structural problem which may have undermined their profit base and lost them their competitive edge in the credit market. As we mentioned earlier, it might be self-evident that the undermined profit base would hinder their market penetration. However, under the imperfect information paradigm, Indonesia's Islamic banks are not to be blamed for their credit rationing; rather, we should ask why these banks are not given adequate bank rent opportunities.

3. A need for Islamic bank rent opportunities

Several approaches have attempted to explain the low level of Islamic financial deepening and the recent slow-paced growth of Indonesian Islamic banking. As Abduh and Omar (2012) insist, economic growth is a major factor that determines the development of Islamic banking. However, we should ask why Indonesia's Islamic banking has stagnated while its conventional banking has been expanding under the same economic circumstance.

One explanation is that the customer's preference and saving behaviour is a critical factor that can determine the development of Islamic banking. Kasri and Kassim (2009) investigated Indonesian Islamic banks' customer behaviour in placing deposits. They investigated the real rate of return on Islamic deposits, the interest rate on conventional deposits, and the real income and number of Islamic bank branches as the factors which determine the level of savings in Islamic banks. Kasri and Kassim find that the level of Islamic bank deposits is positively correlated with the rate of return on Islamic deposits, and negatively correlated with the rate of interest offered by conventional banks if Islamic banks fail to follow it. This is the "displaced commercial risk" by "rational Muslim depositors' behaviour" (ibid.). This is a strong counterargument to Lindsey (2012), who states that the initiatives are predominantly aimed at co-opting the Muslim community – for whom only the strength of *Shari'ah* compliance matters – as potential customers. The rational Muslim depositors' behaviour hypothesis, however, does not fully explain the extraordinarily low level of Islamic financial deepening, because Indonesia's Islamic banks seem to attract their depositors by offering a rate which is still competitive with that offered by conventional banks, as discussed in Chapter 3 (see Table 3.7).

Some scholars are concerned about public awareness of Islamic banking services as the key factor in fostering the growth of Islamic banks in Indonesia (Zubair, 2008; Ismal, 2014). Sari et al. (2016) point out the lack of trust among consumers and the overall consumer misunderstanding of Islamic banking; hence, public awareness in filling in the gaps would be necessary for the growth of Indonesia's Islamic banking industry. In other words, they point out that Indonesian Islamic banks are still "infant", resulting in a failure of installing sufficient confidence and trust in Islamic banking to compete with conventional banks. However, these approaches do not sufficiently explain why Indonesia's Islamic banks are still in their infancy. In addition, these approaches do not sufficiently explain what caused the recent slowing down of Islamic financial deepening.

A number of studies have highlighted the non-achievement of the target market forecast for Islamic banking in Indonesia, as prepared by Indonesian financial and banking authorities in various scenario projections of the period between 2005 and 2013 (see, for example, Ismal, 2014; Sukmana and Kuswanto, 2015; Ismal and Haryati, 2013). Sukmana and Kuswanto (2015) admit that one of the most important factors in achieving the target of Islamic banking growth in Indonesia is the existence of a government affirmative policy to support the Indonesian Islamic banking industry. They argue that, based on the calculation of their projected scenario, the policies of shifting the pilgrimage (*Hajj*) funds – which were previously deposited in the conventional banks – to the Islamic banks and the placement of a national government budget in the Islamic banks were two critical factors for significantly increasing Islamic banking's market share. However, this conclusion does not seem to answer the fundamental problem of how Islamic banks in Indonesia can sustainably have a profit accumulation base and leverage Islamic banking business capabilities to increase their market share in the long run.

As we discussed in Section 2, under the imperfect information paradigm, banks must earn a rent (surplus) to create and maintain their franchise value. It is justifiable if a protective framework for creating the bank rent opportunity would bring a positive outcome (rent effect) of mediating more financial resources and of expanding the office-branch network to facilitate users' access. Lai (2014) attempts to justify the Malaysian governmental initiative of incubating infant Islamic banks under a protective financial architecture to strengthen Malaysia's position as a key player in the international financial hub. However, this argument does not sufficiently address how to measure the economic benefit of the protective financial architecture and does not clearly mention the duration of the protection period.

How much do Islamic banks have to earn in rent to maintain their reputation as prudent and *Shari'ah*-compliant fund providers? Suzuki and Uddin (2014) propose a new concept of Islamic bank rent that Islamic banks must earn. According to them, Islamic bank rent is defined as

> the extra profits enough to compensate for the unexpected loss and the displaced commercial risk to which Islamic banks are facing; in other words, as the excess profits required for maintaining their franchise value and reputation as prudent Shari'ah-compliant lenders.
>
> (ibid., pp. 6–7)

Spread earned by Islamic banks = (*risk-adjusted*) *risk premium* + α
where *spread* = *rate of profit received* − *rate of profit paid*

Suzuki and Uddin (2014) assume that both conventional and Islamic banks seek a risk-adjusted premium in the lending business. Basically, both types of bank are exposed to an identical risk and uncertainty in their competitive credit market. Yet, Islamic banks are considered as being exposed to a unique risk and uncertainty under the profit-and-loss-sharing (PLS) mode. Also, Islamic banks are required to pay a transaction cost for *Shari'ah* compliance to maintain their reputation and to avoid a displaced commercial risk, in which their funds could be withdrawn by depositors if they lose their reputation as *Shari'ah*-compliant fund providers. Thus, it is arguable that Islamic banks need to earn an extra profit (α in the above equation) to maintain their franchise value as prudent *Shari'ah*-compliant lenders. Suzuki and Uddin define α as Islamic bank rent in terms of the extra profit to compensate for the PLS risk and the transaction cost for *Shari'ah* compliance.

If this Islamic bank rent hypothesis is held, Islamic banks must seek a larger spread of margin than conventional banks. Alternatively, as Suzuki and Uddin (2014) suggest, Islamic banks could select low-risk assets for their portfolio so far as the risk-adjusted return is still at a satisfactory level. (Note: according to them, this is an explanation of the mechanism causing the *murabaha* syndrome of concentrating on asset-based financing.) Or, in the competitive market with conventional banks, the profit margin of Islamic banks could be so squeezed by the costs that they would have to pay for their *Shari'ah* compliance. The case of Indonesia's Islamic banks which suffered from lower profitability in comparison with conventional banks, as we analysed in Chapter 3, may endorse this hypothesis.

From a *Shari'ah* perspective, the rate of profit should be determined by mutual consent (Holy Qur'an 4:29: "…do not consume one another's wealth unjustly but only [in lawful] business by mutual consent…"; see also IDB and IFA, 2000, p. 93). On the other hand, Ahmed (2012), while drawing on the NIE approach, indicates that as a result of failing to institutionalize an adequate sanction mechanism, unproductive rent-seeking and "opportunistic" behaviour distort the economic activities even upon genuine Islamic economics objectives. He insists that it is impossible to attain the ideal goals without the establishment of formal rules in accordance with Islamic principles. Grais (2008) emphasizes the importance of setting up regulatory and institutional frameworks in supporting the growth of Islamic finance worldwide. He argues that the policy and institutional challenges faced by the current development of Islamic banks include the preparation of a legal and regulatory framework for improving the access to market information and enhancing the financial infrastructure (ibid., p. 22).

Apparently, the Indonesian regulators failed to (or did not even attempt to) institutionalize a profit base for incubating Indonesian Islamic banks by giving them an appropriate incentive to become prudent fund providers/monitors, ideally while complying with *Shari'ah* rules. Rather, the government of Indonesia has encouraged a free and competitive credit market among conventional and Islamic banks. If the Islamic bank rent hypothesis is held, the governmental "neoliberal" policy would amount to be harsh on Indonesia's Islamic banking industry.

4. Concluding comments

We looked at the important role of financial sector rent as the incentive for banks to mediate financial resources (to reduce credit rationing under the imperfect information paradigm). The bank rent opportunity can function as the rent for learning to catch up and improve the skills and capacity for credit risk management. We also touched on the expected rent effect by the financial restraint policy.

Basically, the infrastructure of Islamic finance is necessary for facilitating the investment and economic transactions by Muslim depositors and investors. If the infrastructure were not available, they would have to pay more transaction costs for *Shari'ah* compliance at an individual level. If they were aware (or unsure) that proceeds from their investment had not complied with *Shari'ah* principles, some Muslim investors would consider "purification" of their proceeds, for instance, by donating them to charity or *zakat* institutions. This circumstance may discourage them from engaging in investment. In other words, the infrastructure of Islamic finance would possibly mobilize more funds from Muslim investors, which would also contribute to national economic growth. The governmental initiatives for developing the infrastructure of Islamic finance are expected to reduce the seemingly high transaction costs of *Shari'ah* compliance at an individual level in Indonesia.

It is worth noting that the rate of financial deepening in Indonesia is categorized at a lower level compared to other Southeast Asian countries. According to the *Global Financial Development Report 2019/2020* (World Bank, 2019), the national financial sector in Indonesia reached only 75.1 per cent of GDP (in terms of percentage of private credit by deposit money banks and stock market capitalization to GDP, and averages of values during 2015–2017). This is still far behind other countries such as Singapore (333.1 per cent), Malaysia (244.5 per cent), Philippines (122.7 per cent), and Thailand (212.3 per cent). This suggests that the overall financial deepening level in Indonesia is low (another big puzzle for the Indonesian economy; see also Chapter 6, Section 3). We believe that the overall stagnated development of Indonesia's banking industry, including Islamic banking, is attributable to the government's failure to create a profit base for banks to develop their skills and capacity for credit monitoring. In fact, it is hypothesized that the Indonesian economy is still mainly driven by consumption and government spending components. Moreover, the governmental neoliberal banking policy should be critically assessed as well.

References

Abduh, M. and Omar, M.A. (2012) Islamic banking and economic growth: The Indonesian experience, *International Journal of Islamic and Middle Eastern Finance and Management*, *5*(1), pp. 35–47.

Ahmed, H. (2012) The Islamization of economies and knowledge: A New Institutional Economics perspective, *American Journal of Islamic Social Sciences*, *29*(4), pp. 22–45.

Aoki, M. (1994) Monitoring characteristics of the main bank system: An analytical and developmental view, in M. Aoki, H.-K. Kim, and M. Okuno-Fujiwara (Eds) *The Role of Government in East Asian Economic Development: Comparative Institutional Analysis.* Oxford: Clarendon Press, pp. 109–141.

Demsetz, R.S., Marc R.S., and Philip, E.S. (1996) Banks with something to lose: The disciplinary role of franchise value, *Federal Reserve Bank of New York Economic Policy Review*, *2*(2), pp. 1–14.

Grais, W. (2008) Islamic banking: Policy and institutional challenges, *Journal of Islamic Economics, Banking and Finance*, 4(1) (January–April), pp. 14–26.

Hellmann, T., Murdock, K., and Stiglitz, J. (1997) Financial restraint: Toward a new paradigm, in M. Aoki, H.-K. Kim, and M. Okuno-Fujiwara (Eds) *The Role of Government in East Asian Economic Development: Comparative Institutional Analysis.* Oxford: Clarendon Press, pp. 163–207.

Islamic Development Bank (IDB) and Islamic Fiqh Academy (IFA). (2000) *Resolutions and Recommendation of the Council of Islamic Fiqh Academy 1985–2000.* Jeddah: IDB and IFA.

Ismal, R. (2014) Indonesia, the resilience and prospects of Islamic banking, in S. Thiagaraja et al. (Eds) *The Islamic Finance Handbook, A Practitioner's Guide to the Global Market.* Singapore: John Wiley and Sons, pp. 155–173.

Ismal, R. and Haryati, R. (2013) The optimal and decreasing growth rate of the Islamic banking industry, *Qualitative Research in Financial Markets*, *5*(3), pp. 229–243.

Kasri, R.A. and Kassim S.H. (2009) Empirical determinants of saving in the Islamic banks: Evidence from Indonesia, *Islamic Economics*, *22*(2), pp. 3–23.

Khan, M. (2000) Rents, efficiency and growth, in M. Khan and J.K. Sundaram (Eds), *Rents, Rent-seeking and Economic Development: Theory and Evidence in Asia.* Cambridge: Cambridge University Press, pp. 21–69.

Lai, J. (2014) Industrial policy and Islamic finance, *New Political Economy*, *20*(2), pp. 178–198.

Lindsey, T. (2012). Between piety and prudence: State Syariah and the regulation of Islamic banking in Indonesia, *Sydney Law Review*, *34*(107), pp. 1–16.

Sari, M.D., Bahari, Z., and Hamat, Z. (2016) History of Islamic bank in Indonesia: Issues behind its establishment, *International Journal of Finance and Banking Research*, *2*(5), pp. 178–184. doi: 10.11648/j.ijfbr.20160205.13

Stiglitz, J.E. (1994) The role of the state in financial markets, in M. Bruno and B. Pleskovic (Eds) *Proceedings of the World Bank Annual Conference on Development Economics, 1993: Supplement to the World Bank Economic Review and the World Bank Research Observer.* Washington, D.C.: World Bank, pp. 19–52.

Stiglitz, J.E. and Weiss, A. (1981) Credit rationing in markets with imperfect information, *The American Economic Review*, *71*(3), pp. 393–410.

Sukmana, R. and Kuswanto, H. (2015) Assessment on the Islamic banking market share projection by Bank Indonesia and proposed methods, *Journal of Islamic Monetary Economics and Finance*, *1*(1), 107–133.

Suzuki, Y. (2011) *Japan's Financial Slump: Collapse of the Monitoring System under Institutional and Transition Failures.* Basingstoke, UK: Palgrave Macmillan.

Suzuki, Y. and Adhikary, B.K. (2009) A "bank rent" approach to understanding the development of the banking system in Bangladesh, *Contemporary South Asia*, *18*(2), pp. 155–173.

Suzuki, Y., Miah, M.D., and Wanniarachchige, M.K. (2017) Overview of theories of financial sector rent and bank rent opportunities: A critical view, in Y. Suzuki, M.D.

Miah, M.K. Wanniarachchige, and S.M.S. Uddin (Eds) *Banking and Economic Rent in Asia: Rent Effects, Financial Fragility, and Economic Development*. Abingdon, UK: Routledge, pp. 13–25.

Suzuki, Y. and Uddin, S.M.S. (2014) Islamic bank rent: A case study of Islamic banking in Bangladesh, *International Journal of Islamic and Middle Eastern Finance and Management*, *7*(2), pp. 170–181.

Wanniarachchige, M.K. (2017) Creating bank rent in developing countries: An integrated model, in Y. Suzuki, M.D. Miah, M.K. Wanniarachchige, and S.M.S. Uddin (Eds.) *Banking and Economic Rent in Asia: Rent Effects, Financial Fragility, and Economic Development*. Abingdon, UK: Routledge, pp. 38–57.

World Bank. (2019) *Global Financial Development Report 2019/2020: Bank Regulation and Supervision a Decade after the Global Financial Crisis*. Washington, DC: World Bank.

Zubair, M.K. (2008) Acceleration of the growth of Islamic banking in Indonesia, *Journal Millah*, *8*(1), pp. 1–19.

5 Comparative study of Islamic banking regulation frameworks in Indonesia and Malaysia

1. Introduction

Why has Indonesia failed to catch up with Malaysia, a close neighbouring Muslim country that has somewhat successfully proceeded with the Islamization of its own banking industry? What were the secrets for the successful development of Malaysia's Islamic banking? It is time to tackle Puzzle 2. We gave an overview of the genesis and the socio-political context of Indonesia's Islamic banking industry in Chapter 2, Sections 3 and 4. This chapter primarily aims to look at Malaysia's Islamic banking industry for a better understanding of its history, socio-economic background, and regulatory framework. We hypothesize that the Malaysian government offered an initiative for incubating its Islamic banks as well as for developing the infrastructure of Islamic banking. Needless to say, there are differences between the two financial systems, which are a result of their evolution and adaptation to their surrounding environments. We recognize the fundamental limitation in the comparative study; however, although the different financial systems have diverse histories, technologies, and attitudes towards risk-taking, we believe they have a common factor, which is to ensure financial efficiency within a geographical region.

There are two models in conducting the Islamization of the banking industry through its own economic programmes in Muslim countries (Wibisono, 2009). The first model aims to create a single fully-fledged Islamic financial system by restructuring the national banking system. This is observed, for instance, in Sudan, Iran, and Pakistan, where only Islamic banking is allowed and regulated under the policy of Islamization. The second model is called a dual banking system. Under this system, Islamic banks operate in parallel with conventional banks under identical banking regulations at national level. This model is being applied in many countries including Saudi Arabia, Bangladesh, Egypt, Jordan, Kuwait, and Bahrain, as well as Indonesia and Malaysia. Noticeably, as argued by Chapra and Khan (2000) as well as by Wibisono (2009), the regulatory framework is a crucial factor in shaping the development of Islamic banking under any model.

The rest of this chapter is organized as follows. Section 2 gives an overview of the regulatory framework of Islamic banking in Indonesia to clarify its unique features. Sections 3 and 4 discuss the key factors in the incubation of Malaysia's Islamic banks. A protective regulatory framework for Islamic banking is argued for. Section 5 summarizes the key factors of well-incubated Malaysian Islamic banks along with those of badly incubated Indonesian Islamic banks.

2. The development and regulatory framework of Islamic banking in Indonesia

Dual banking system

In Indonesia, as referred to in Chapter 2, Section 3, a new stage began with the enactment of Act No. 10 Year 1998, an amendment to Act No. 7 Year 1992, which allowed the conventional banks to open Islamic banking windows or divisions (*Unit Usaha Syariah*/UUS). This new regulation subsequently triggered the expansion of the Islamic banking industry and also officially recognized the acceptance by Bank Indonesia (BI) of the existence of Islamic banks in the dual banking system.

Act No. 23 Year 1999 concerning BI redefined the central bank's responsibilities to regulation and supervision of the national banking system, including Islamic banks and the Islamic Rural Bank (Bank Perkreditan Rakyat Syariah). We witnessed BI reinforcing its authority in Act No. 3 Year 2004 on the amendment of Act No. 23 Year 1999. BI moved forward to drive the development of Indonesia's Islamic banks using the Islamic office-channelling policy (basically to provide Islamic banking products at conventional banks) based on BI's Regulation (Peraturan Bank Indonesia/PBI) No. 8/3/PBI Year 2006, which allowed cooperation mechanisms of depositor fund collection between the Islamic branch and the conventional branch under the same parent bank.[1] The regulation was then refined through PBI No. 9/7/PBI Year 2007, in which requirements for the opening of the office-channelling funds were relaxed and functions were expanded, by allowing not only depositor fund collection, but also comprehensive provision of financing and financial services to the bank's customers. On 17 June 2008, Islamic Banking Act No. 21 Year 2008 was enacted to clearly endorse that the banks in Indonesia comprise of two types, conventional and Islamic banks. Table 5.1 highlights the important milestones of policy and regulation on the development of Islamic banking in Indonesia.

Guidance from Bank Indonesia

To encourage all the stakeholders in the Islamic banking industry to determine their long-term strategic programmes for expanding their market share, BI issued in 2002 a series of strategic policy initiatives in the *Blueprint of the Development of Islamic Banking Industry 2002 to 2015*. In general, this blueprint document proposes six initiative programmes to be implemented within ten years (2005–2015): (1) increasing *Shari'ah* compliance; (2) increasing the quality of prudential banking operations; (3) increasing operational efficiency and competitiveness;

Table 5.1 Important milestones of policy and regulation in the development of Indonesia's Islamic banking

Year	*Banking policies and regulations*
1980s	The inception of several microfinance institutions and cooperatives which operated based on Islamic principles.
1990	Indonesian Ulama Council (Majelis Ulama Indonesia/MUI) held a forum on interest and banking, with the theme "The problems of prohibition of interest and banking".
1992	The enactment of Banking Act No. 7 Year 1992, recognizing profit-sharing banking.
1992	The first Islamic bank, PT Bank Muamalat Indonesia (BMI), officially started its operation.
1998	The government approved the dual banking system in Indonesia through the Banking Act No. 10 Year 1998, which allowed for *Shari'ah* windows operations.
1999	The establishment of the National *Shari'ah* Board (Dewan Syariah Nasional/ DSN) in accordance with Decree No. 754 /MUI /II/1999.
2003	Issuance of *fatwa* by MUI on bank interest, considered as unlawful (prohibited) to the Muslim.
2008	The enactment of Islamic Banking Act No. 21 Year 2008. It clearly endorses that banks in Indonesia comprise of two types, conventional banks and Islamic.
2011	The enactment of Act No. 21 Year 2011 regarding the Financial Services Authority (FSA) on 17 October 2011. The FSA became the new banking supervisor and authority for the banking and financial industry in Indonesia.
2015	The FSA issued the *Roadmap of Indonesian Islamic Banking 2015–2019.*
2016	The establishment of the National Committee for Islamic Finance (Komite Nasional Keuangan Syariah/KNK) in accordance with President's Regulation No. 91 Year 2016 dated 3 November 2016, launched by the President of the Republic of Indonesia on 24 July 2017.
2020	The extending and changing nomenclature of KNKS to National Committee for Islamic Economics and Finance (Komite Nasional Ekonomi dan Keuangan Syariah/KNEKS) in accordance with President's Regulation No. 28 Year 2020, dated 10 February 2020.

Source: From various sources, constructed by the authors.

(4) increasing the stability of the banking system; (5) increasing the expertise and quality of human resources; and (6) optimizing the social role of Islamic banks in developing small and medium enterprises (BI, 2006).

In 2008, BI issued another grand strategy for the development of the Islamic banking industry, namely the Market Development Strategic Programme (MDSP) (Markplus and BI, 2008; Ismal, 2011). The programme document basically contained the marketing strategy that should be implemented by the regulators and the Islamic banks to boost the market share of Islamic banking in Indonesia. The MDSP recommendations are: (1) to position the industry as the most attractive one and the leader among the ASEAN countries in 2009 and 2010; (2) to create a new image of Islamic banks which is inclusive and universal;

(3) to accurately map Islamic banking's potential market; (4) to develop Islamic banking products; (5) to improve banking services and; (6) to communicate the new position of Islamic banks as being beyond banking (Markplus and BI, 2008).

We acknowledge that one of the important policies related to efforts in increasing the market share of the Indonesian Islamic banks is BI's Islamic Banking Accelerated Programmes 2007–2008 (Program Akselerasi Perbankan Syariah) which was included as a policy package in the Islamic Banking Outlook 2007. Basically, the purpose of the Islamic Banking Accelerated Programmes 2007–2008 is the achievement of Islamic banking share of 5.25 per cent of the total assets in the Indonesian banking industry by the end of 2008, while maintaining prudent banking principles and adherence to Islamic principles. This policy focused on achieving quantitative targets through a ground-breaking package of policy and programme initiatives that can provide significant bank asset growth changes in the short term (BI, 2006).

The Islamic Banking Accelerated Programmes 2007–2008 had six pillars, namely: (1) to strengthen institutional aspects of the Islamic banks; (2) to develop Islamic banks' products and services; (3) to intensify public awareness of and strategic alliance with Islamic banking; (4) to increase the role of government and strengthen the legal framework for Islamic banking; (5) to strengthen Islamic banks' human resources; and (6) to tighten the supervision of Islamic banks (BI, 2006).

BI (2006) describes, in a broad sense, the Islamic Banking Accelerated Programmes 2007–2008 as being conducted through three main functions. Firstly, the socialization of Islamic banking in the community should be more intensive to increase bank customers' understanding of Islamic banking and finance operations and products. Secondly, innovation should be encouraged and Islamic banks' products and services expanded to fulfil demand in society. Thirdly, the central bank should be more active in supporting the capital inflow of foreign investment funds through Islamic financial instruments. Despite these efforts, the targeted market share was not achieved.

Financial Services Authority (FSA)

The FSA was established by Act No. 21 Year 2011 concerning FSA, and aimed to perform its function as an independent integrated regulatory and supervisory body for the whole financial industry in Indonesia. According to Article 4, Act No. 21 Year 2011, the establishment of the FSA was intended to ensure that the overall activities in the financial services industry are conducted in a well-managed and accountable manner; it aims to realize a sustainable and stable financial system, and to accomplish protection for consumers and public interests.

According to Article 6 of Act No. 21 Year 2011, the FSA started out acting as a regulator and supervisor of all the banking regulations pertaining to individual banks, to achieve and maintain the soundness of those individual banks. With regard to Islamic banking operations, the FSA performs its functions to deliver the licences and articles of association/approval and to maintain the soundness and prudential aspects of the supervised Islamic banks.

In 2015, the FSA issued the *Roadmap of Indonesian Islamic Banking 2015–2019*. Within this strategic document, the vision for the development of Indonesian Islamic banks was formulated as "Actualizing Islamic banking that gives significant contributions to sustainable economic growth, equitable development, financial system stability, and high competitiveness". Furthermore, this development vision was translated into policy directions, work programmes, and time-scheduled implementations. Accordingly, there were seven policy directions: (1) to strengthen policy synergy between the authority and government and other stakeholders; (2) to strengthen capital and business scales as well as enhancing efficiency; (3) to improve funding structure by supporting the expansion of financing segments; (4) to improve service quality and product diversity; (5) to improve size and quality of human resources and information and technology; (6) to enhance public literacy and preferences; and (7) to strengthen and harmonize regulations and supervision (FSA, 2015, pp. xv–xvi). Yet, at the point of writing, the growth of Indonesia's Islamic banking had slowed down and is still stagnant.

In 2017, the FSA issued the *Roadmap of Indonesian Islamic Finance 2015–2019*, which was purposed to integrate three roadmaps of the Islamic financial industry in Indonesia: the Islamic banking roadmap, the Islamic capital market roadmap, and the non-bank Islamic financial institutions roadmap. Although this roadmap has set its strategic objectives comprehensively to enhance the inclusivity of the Islamic financial services industry, this document has not sufficiently presented any strategic plan to create the incentives needed by the market players in the Islamic financial industry.

3. National Committee for Islamic Economics and Finance

In 2016, in accordance with President's Regulation No. 91 Year 2016 dated 3 November 2016, the Indonesian government established the National Committee for Islamic Finance (Komite Nasional Keuangan Syariah/KNKS). This committee was launched by the President of the Republic of Indonesia on 24 July 2017. In brief, this committee was assigned to accelerate, expand, and advance the development of Islamic finance in supporting the national economy. Two major documents as the guidelines for Islamic economic and financial development were released by the KNKS in collaboration with the Ministry of National Development Planning/National Development Planning Agency (Badan Perencanaan Pembangunan Nasional/ Bappenas): the *Indonesian Islamic Financial Architecture Masterplan* (Bappenas, 2015) and the *Indonesian Islamic Economics Masterplan 2019–2024* (Bappenas, 2018).

Subsequently, in 2020, based on President's Regulation No. 28 Year 2020 dated 10 February 2020, the nomenclature of KNKS was changed by the government to the National Committee for Islamic Economics and Finance (Komite Nasional Ekonomi dan Keuangan Syariah/KNEKS). According to this regulation, KNEKS is expected to build a broader Islamic economic ecosystem that includes *halal* industry product development, Islamic finance development, and the expansion of *Shari'ah* business and Islamic social funds (*zakat*, *waqf*, and Islamic philanthropy development).

Unique features of Indonesian Islamic banking

Many researchers and scholars, including Wibisono (2009), Alamsyah (2012), and Ismal (2013), highlight the unique characteristics of Indonesia's Islamic banking industry in comparison to other countries. Here, let us summarize the salient features in Indonesian Islamic banking.

First, the impetus for establishing Islamic banking in Indonesia was initiated at a grassroots level of demand for Islamic financial institutions based on free-of-interest banking and compliance with *Shari'ah* principles in business (Islamic jurisprudence/*Fiqh al Muamalah*). Looking at the historical background of the establishment of Indonesia's Islamic banking, we recognize that the related regulations and policies were influenced by the bottom-up (alternatively, we may say, "not centralized") voice in which the Muslim community specifically played a role in initiating or encouraging the government to support the development of Islamic banking. We assume, however, that the decentralized structure of political power or the weak coordination of the bottom-up voices may have led to the lack of leadership, resulting in a failure to incubate the infant Islamic banking industry in Indonesia.

Second, as we discussed in Chapter 3, Indonesia's Islamic banks are focused on penetrating consumer finance and are apparently hesitant to delve more into the corporate financing market or to enter into the investment banking business in the profit-and-loss-sharing (PLS) mode. One should be reminded here that the strategy of Indonesian Islamic banks in concentrating on consumer finance apparently did not always bring a satisfactory profit base. On the other hand, the business in PLS mode may rely heavily on "*Shari'ah* loyalist" bank customers. The number of that type of customer in Indonesia is not yet enough for its Islamic banks to enter into the PLS mode (this issue will be discussed in Chapter 7).

Third, as we saw earlier, while the Indonesian government has taken the initiative in setting up various regulations related to Islamic banking and financial institutions, these regulations were noticeably not well-coordinated under the decentralized structure of decision-making in the government. Obviously, Indonesia's Islamic banking industry has been shaped by different governmental and industrial heads, such as BI, the FSA, Ministry of Finance (MOF), Indonesia Deposit Insurance Corporation (Lembaga Penjamin Simpanan), National *Shari'ah* Board (Dewan Syariah Nasional/DSN), Ministry of Religious Affairs, National Zakat Board (Badan Amil Zakat), the Indonesian Institute of Accountants, and so on.

We can raise the case of double tax imposition on *murabaha* transactions as an example of the problematic rent-seeking or slow decision-making in regulating Islamic banking. In fact, it took approximately 17 years since the first Islamic bank was established in 1992 until the double tax imposition on *murabaha* transactions was finally abolished with the enactment of Act No. 42 Year 2009 on Tax Neutrality. This condition was of course very detrimental to the Islamic banks' business since about 50 per cent of the revenue was generated from the *murabaha* financing mode (Wibisono, 2009). A senior researcher at BI reveals through our interview that the delay in implementing public policies in the Islamic financial sector is attributable mainly to the rent-seeking among the different heads in the government and industry bodies (see Chapter 9 for the details).

Fourth, the DSN, or National *Shari'ah* Board, is independent from the financial authorities such as the central bank (BI) or the FSA. The DSN was established by the Indonesian Ulama Council (Majelis Ulama Indonesia/MUI) in accordance with Decree No. 754/MUI/II/1999 Year 1999. This governance structure in Indonesia is in sharp contrast to that in Malaysia, where the National *Shari'ah* Advisory Council (NSAC), as the *Shari'ah* standards and regulatory body, is under the control of Bank Negara Malaysia (BNM, the central bank). From the perspective of governance structure, the NSAC is not perfectly independent from BNM.

The main responsibility of the DSN is to support the governance of the Islamic banking and finance industries from the perspective of *Shari'ah* compliance. In doing so, the DSN has an important role in creating trust and confidence in the general public so that they may receive financial services from *Shari'ah*-compliant financial institutions. For fulfilling this responsibility and its role, independence is required and desirable from the viewpoint of governance structure. However, higher transaction costs for coordinating with the regulators are borne as a by-product in Indonesia, including those incurred by the time-consuming coordination for ensuring coherence between the *fatwa* issued by the DSN and the banking policy direction issued by the financial authorities (see Chapter 9 for further discussion).

4. The development and regulatory framework of Islamic banking in Malaysia

Let us look at the features in the regulatory framework of Islamic banking in Malaysia. According to Lai (2015), the development of Islamic finance and banking in Malaysia has gone through an evolutionary process from the emergence and infant industry protectionism phases (1980s–1990s), to the expansionary phase and take-off stage (1993–2010), and to consolidation of the market and becoming a key player as an international hub for global Islamic finance (2011 to present). As a whole, we see that the establishment and development of Islamic banking in Malaysia is a government-driven (top-down or centralized) strategic policy in supporting the Islamization agenda in social and political spheres. Obviously, it is reflected in the government's commitment to develop its Islamic banking and finance industry by establishing a robust regulatory and supervisory framework. Also, the Malaysian government had prepared adequate economic policies to provide incentives and protection in ensuring the

Table 5.2 Highlights of important milestones in Malaysian Islamic banking policies and regulations

Year	*Banking policies and regulations*
1983	On 7 April 1983, the Malaysian government enacted the Islamic Banking Act. The first Islamic commercial bank in Malaysia, Bank Islam Malaysia Berhad (BIMB), was established.
1983	The Malaysian government ratified the Government Investment Act, which authorized it to be able to issue government investment facilities based on *Shari'ah* principles.
1984	The Malaysian government issued the *Takaful* (Insurance) Act.
1993	On 4 March 1993, the Malaysian government introduced the Interest-free Banking System (IFBS, Skim Perbankan Tanpa Faedah/SPTF). Under this policy, the conventional banks are allowed to offer Islamic banking products.
1994	On 4 January 1994, the government established the Islamic Interbank Money Market.
1997	On 1 May 1997, the government established the National *Shari'ah* Advisory Council (NSAC).
2001	The government issued the Financial Sector Master Plan that covered the period of 2001–2011.
2011	The government issued the Financial Sector Blueprint that covered the subsequent decade, 2011–2020.
2013	The amalgamation of six Acts into new two Acts, namely the Financial Services Act 2013 and the Islamic Financial Services Act 2013.

Source: From various sources, constructed by the authors.

sustainability of the development of the Islamic finance and banking industry in the early stages of its establishment (Othman et al., 2017). Table 5.2 presents the important milestones of policy and regulation in the development of Malaysian Islamic banking.

Centralized structure in Islamic banking

On 7 April 1983, the Malaysian government enacted the Islamic Banking Act (IBA). Under the IBA, the government had authorized the BNM, the central bank, to act as an authority and supervisor for Islamic banking operations. Also in 1983, the Malaysian government ratified the Government Investment Act, which authorized the government to issue government investment facilities, a type of marketable securities based on *Shari'ah* principles.

In 1983, concurrently with the enactment of the IBA, the first Islamic commercial bank in Malaysia, Bank Islam Malaysia (BIMB), was established. In fact, BIMB is considered as a semi-public sector financial institution as its initial paid-up capital was raised from a variety of state financial sources, such as the Government of Malaysia, Lembaga Tabung Haji, state religious councils, state religious agencies, and other federal agencies, as well as Muslim community welfare organizations (Lai, 2015; Othman et al., 2017). Then, in 1984, the Malaysian government issued the *Takaful* (Insurance) Act, which became the foundation of the Islamic insurance industry, operated according to *Shari'ah* principles. The Malaysian government believes the Islamic insurance industry is one of the important sectors in supporting the development of the Islamic banking sector.

Until the end of the emergence phase and infant industry protectionism period (1980s–1990s), we observe that the direction of the Malaysian government policy of Islamic banking development was characterized by an incubation of the infant industry, and by an intervention policy in the form of protectionism for the new Islamic bank just established. We see that the first Islamic bank had an effective monopoly in the market (Lai, 2015).

From the early 1990s, the development of Islamic banking in Malaysia had moved toward the expansionary and take-off stage (1993–2010). BNM took a keen interest to make a breakthrough in the monopoly market condition of Islamic banking by choosing to adopt the Islamic windows scheme, as this is leveraged on the existing branch network and infrastructure of the conventional banks and is a cheaper and faster way to facilitate the growth of Islamic banking (Lai, 2015).

On 4 March 1993, the Malaysian government introduced the Interest-Free Banking System (IFBS, Skim Perbankan Tanpa Faedah/SPTF). Under this system, conventional banks are allowed to offer Islamic banking products. This synergized model is known as the "Islamic bank windows". Obviously, this policy effectively promoted the growth of Malaysia's Islamic banking industry since the conventional bank branches and networks were utilized to serve Islamic banking products. We should note that the government's policy in this regard was conducted in a prudent and gradual manner, for instance in encouraging the Islamic windows programme through the IFBS, in which the government's preliminary emphasis was on removing the element of interest from banking rather than the implementation of a systematically fleshed-out Islamic financial system in the national economy.

Furthermore, the Malaysian government took an institutional development initiative which was significantly important to the Islamic banking and finance industry, that is, the establishment of both the Islamic Interbank Money Market on 4 January 1994 and the NSAC on 1 May 1997.

The Asian financial crisis in 1997, which hit the Malaysian economy, was an epoch-making development in Malaysia's Islamic banking. The Malaysian government worked to increase the contribution of foreign direct investment as an important driver of its economic growth and to organize the mix of financial sector reform in the wake of the crisis. This effort pushed the policy-makers and the financial authority to identify the Islamic banking sector not only as a means to re-energize its financial system, but also as a new source of wealth for the domestic economy (Lai, 2015, 2012). In addition, the development of Malaysia's Islamic banking obtained its momentum from the Malaysian political situation, brought by the leadership of the former Prime Minister Mahathir Mohamad (Alim, 2014). The Malaysian government had obviously provided very substantial support and privileges to the interests of the Malays as a protection for their "*Bumiputera* welfare" (economic welfare of the Malays in Malaysia). This affirmative policy was part of the implementation of the well-known New Economic Policy from 1970 to the 1990s (Gomez and Jomo, 1997; Haneef, 2001; Lai, 2015). Perhaps the combination of strong leadership from the duo of former Prime Minister Mahathir Mohamad and former Deputy Prime Minister Anwar Ibrahim in the early 1990s worked well as an effective state intervention in developing the Islamic finance and banking industry in the Muslim world.

BNM issued the licence for a second fully-fledged Islamic bank in 1999, Bank Bumi Muamalat (BBM). Similarly, in the case of the establishment of BIMB, the first Islamic bank in Malaysia, the Malaysian government was actively involved in the establishment of BBM. Substantially, BBM was the result of a merger of two conventional banks, Commerce Asset-Holding and Bank Bumiputra Malaysia, a government-owned bank. These newly merged banks were spun off into a new Islamic commercial bank (Lai, 2015).

In 2013, in order to enhance its financial stability and protect the rights and interests of financial customers, BNM took the initiative to review its existing regulatory frameworks related to the financial system, including the Banking and Financial Act 1989, Insurance Act 1996, Payment Act 2003, Exchange Control Act 1953, IBA 1983, and *Takaful* Act 1984. This assessment resulted in accomplishing the amalgamation and robust policy direction into new two Acts, namely the Financial Services Act 2013 and Islamic Financial Services Act 2013 (Othman et al., 2017).

Successful Islamic financial deepening

At the end of 2007, Malaysia's Islamic banking had about 15 per cent of market share in the national banking industry, a significant increase from 6 per cent in the mid-1990s (Lai, 2015). As of 31 December 2010, the total assets of Islamic banks in Malaysia occupied 20.7 per cent (BNM, 2011). It is reported that at the second quarter of 2018, the total assets of Islamic banking in Malaysia had reached 26.5 per cent of the entire banking system (IFSB, 2019).

Krasicka and Nowak (2012) point out two key factors behind the significant increase of Malaysia's Islamic banks' market share under a dual banking system. Firstly, achieving economies of scale by the utilization of the common platform of the conventional banks' infrastructure and network by the Islamic banking windows had a substantial impact on accelerating Islamic banks' services, at the lowest cost and within the shortest timeframe. Secondly, the Malaysian government supported Islamic banks with substantial tax and fiscal incentives to give them the rent opportunity to catch up with conventional banks. The Malaysian government made clear and immediate policies to enforce implementation for the avoidance of double tax and stamp duties for Islamic banks' transactions and products/services.

Since entering the market consolidation stage in 2011, Malaysia is now a key player in becoming an international financial global hub for Islamic finance (Lai, 2015). According to the *Financial Sector Blueprint* covering the subsequent decade (2011–2020), Islamic banking is expected to account for 40 per cent of the total financing by 2020 (BNM, 2011a).

The Malaysian government continues to provide a protective framework for Islamic banks, especially in the country's strategy to realize the vision of Malaysia as the International Islamic Finance Centre (MIFC) (PWC, 2006; Chang, 2009). For instance, the Malaysian government had provided income tax exemption for ten years (effective since 2007) for banks/windows formed under the IBA 1983 for the income derived from the activities of Islamic banking in foreign currencies, including transactions with Malaysian citizens. Furthermore, the tax-free income can be repatriated to banks' shareholders as a tax-free dividend. Banks' shareholders, in the form of corporations, can once again repatriate that income as tax-free dividends to shareholders (second-tier tax-exempt dividend).

In another example, there is an ownership limit imposed on financial institutions (the foreign equity participation of up to 49 per cent was relaxed to 70 per cent in 2009). This discretion was permitted only for Islamic banking subsidiaries and new *Takaful* companies. This was not given to conventional banks that only had authorization for ownership limits for foreign investors of up to 30 per cent (Lai, 2015).

At the individual level, the Malaysian government offers relief of up to RM 5,000 per year in tuition for Islamic finance programmes at local colleges approved by BNM and the Securities Commission, including the International Centre for Education in Islamic Finance (INCEIF). For corporations, effective since 2007, the incentives are given in the form of a double deduction on expenses for the employees in Islamic banking and finance courses at national universities also approved by BNM, the Securities Commission, and the INCEIF (PWC, 2006; Chang, 2009).

The exemption of stamp duty (up to 100 per cent and valid for ten years) is given on instruments denominated in foreign currency held by Islamic banks, and foreign exchange instruments relating to *Shari'ah* securities denominated in ringgit or foreign currency. The Malaysian government also provided tax exemptions to the consultancy fees received by foreign experts who provided consultancy services for Islamic finance. The foreign experts must be verified by the MIFC based in Malaysia. This incentive was effective from 2007 until the end of 2016 (PWC, 2006; Chang, 2009).

5. Summary: A comparison of important features on Islamic banking development in Indonesia and Malaysia

Having compared the regulatory framework in both countries, we note that the Malaysian government has provided a protective and supportive framework of giving rent opportunities to infant Islamic banks to catch up with conventional banks, while the Indonesian government has not prepared such a protective and supportive framework. The dynamics of the socio-political context in Indonesia and Malaysia have certainly influenced the process of regulatory development in each country.

Malaysian policies were conducted under the framework of a federal representative democratic constitutional monarchy. The Constitution of Malaysia, Article 3: The State Religion, Clause 1, states: "Islam is the religion of the Federation; but other religions may be practiced in peace and harmony in any part of the Federation". Under the political structure, there was consensus to infuse Islamic law principles into the preparation and application of regulations in the political constellation, which was supported by the general public in Malaysia (Fernando, 2006). Obviously, Malaysian financial authorities attempted to be consistent in enacting relevant laws before the establishment of Islamic financial institutions (Othman et al., 2017).

In contrast, although the majority in the demographic composition is occupied by Muslims, the Republic of Indonesia took a different way of seeking a national consensus in the nexus of politics and religion. The founding fathers of the Republic, in the preparations for Indonesian independence in 1945, made and committed to the philosophical fundamentals of the nation state, that is, *Pancasila*. *Pancasila* consists of five principles and contends that they are inseparable and interrelated. The first principle of *Pancasila* is: "Belief in the one and only God". It seems that the founding fathers had a preference that placed the "substantive values" approach of the *Maqashid al Shari'ah* (the objective of *Shari'ah*) as the whole spirit of the constitutional and nation-building construction (Madjid, 1987). *Pancasila* has become the soul of the Indonesian democracy and the guiding principles of national life. This particular philosophical thought was chosen to describe how Indonesia is neither a religious nor a secular state. In fact, in both the Old Order period (1945–1965) under President Sukarno and the New Order period (1966–1998) under President Suharto, the ruling government and parliament handled with care and guardedness the integration of *Shari'ah* concerns into the national legislation system. Extensive efforts to incorporate *Shari'ah* principles into the state laws in the economic and social fields were only made since 1998, after the era of democratization and economic reform, including conducive political and economic reform under the initiatives led by the third president, B.J. Habibie, and his followers.

We are concerned that Indonesian Islamic banking has been unsuccessful in implementing the strategic programme of the massive opening of the UUS to leverage the conventional banking infrastructure. This is in sharp contrast to the case of Malaysia. Although the Indonesian government carried out a dual banking system and provided the opportunity for conventional banks to open Islamic banking windows, the UUS in Indonesia were not fully able to utilize the conventional banking infrastructure since they tend to be hesitant in optimizing the conventional banking infrastructure; this is because the office-channelling facility is rigid and there is no incentive in implementing UUS in conventional banking operations. Through our interviews, senior Islamic bankers in Indonesia admitted that the bank managers of conventional parent banks were not so supportive of this office-channelling strategy, because the output from the UUS was not counted in the assessment of their performance as managers. In contrast, both the CEO of the conventional parent company and the CEO of the UUS are committed to a common vision for the full support of this office-channelling practice in Malaysia. Moreover, the performance of the UUS counts towards the performance of the conventional parent company as well.

In addition, it is worth noting that the Malaysian regulator, BNM, relaxes its tight control in the case of conversion from dual banking with Islamic windows to a fully-fledged Islamic bank, so as to ease the burden of the conversion on the parent company (Othman et al., 2017). In contrast, the Indonesian regulator has tight control, in accordance with Act No. 21 of 2008 regarding Islamic Banking, article 68 paragraph 1, where the type of conventional bank with UUS is strictly required to perform a spin-off accomplishment of its Islamic windows to become a fully-fledged Islamic bank by the end of July 2023 at the latest (see our discussion in Chapter 9).

We should note that Indonesia's Islamic banks were not given an adequate tax and fiscal incentive even in the early stages of their incubation. This is also in sharp contrast with the case of Malaysia. We assume that the Indonesian government failed to (or did not attempt to) create the rent opportunities to be captured by Islamic banks for learning the skills and knowledge in credit risk monitoring to compete with conventional banks. Perhaps, the different paths and regulatory frameworks in incubating the Islamic banking industry in both countries are reflected in each country's social, political, and religious backgrounds. We looked at the socio-political context of Indonesia's Islamic banking in Chapter 2, Section 4.

It appears that Malaysia's centralized (or top-down) incubation of Islamic banking was reflected in its political patronage-client structure of promoting the government's preference for the economic interests of the *Bumiputera* (ethnic Malay people), which is dominated by a Muslim population (Haneef, 2001; Lai, 2015). In contrast, we can see the decentralized or "fragmented" political structure in Indonesia reflected in the slow process of incubating its Islamic banking industry. For instance, the influence on economic policy during the New Order period from 1966 to 1998 by the so-called Berkeley Mafia group in the MOF and the central bank, BI, are widely known. The group, primarily influenced by the Anglo-American neoliberal school of economic thought, was positioned against the interventionist view (see Robison, 1990; Baswir, 2006). The lack of political leadership under a fragmented political structure in Indonesia is also raised as a cause of the slow process.

The government is probably not only to be blamed. It seems that the top executives of Indonesia's Islamic banks have lost their motivation for expanding their operations. Through our interviews with the bank managers of Indonesia's Islamic banks, we find a general mood of giving up (the lack of a "strong will" from the top executives of Islamic banks) in seeking a synergized vision with conventional bank managers in attaining Islamic banking growth.

The adequate preparation of Islamic bank regulations is a challenge for the banking authority to strike a balance between effective supervision, creating a level playing field conducive to all the banks, and encouraging the Islamic banking industry to grow optimally. In the creation of a level playing field for all the banks, the Malaysian "interventionist" model is not always fair, because it may hamper the interests of conventional banks. On the other hand, in the encouragement of the Islamic banking industry to grow optimally, the Indonesian "neoliberal" strategy appears naive.

Note

1 Office-channelling is a terminology that refers to the practice of Indonesian Islamic banks utilizing conventional banks' office networks by the UUS to offer Islamic banking products/services to their customers. The implementation of this office-channelling policy is based on BI Regulation (PBI/BI Regulation) No. 8/3/2006, although this regulation does not explicitly use office-channelling terminology. The official terminology used is *Shari'ah* Services (*Layanan Syariah*), which has been defined as: "the fundraising activities conducted in branch offices or sub-branch offices for and on behalf of the Islamic windows branch office from the identical conventional bank…"

References

Alamsyah, H. (2012) Perkembangan dan prospek perbankan Syariah Indonesia: Tantangan dalam menyongsong MEA 2015. Keynote Speech delivered at *Milad ke-8 Ikatan Ahli Ekonomi Islam (IAEI)* on 13 April 2012.

Alim, E.A. (2014) *Global Leaders in Islamic Finance: Industry Milestones and Reflections.* Singapore: John Wiley and Sons.

Badan Perencanaan Pembangunan Nasional (Bappenas). (2015) *Masterplan Arsitektur Keuangan Syariah di Indonesia.* Jakarta: Bappenas.

Badan Perencanaan Pembangunan Nasional (Bappenas). (2018) *Masterplan Ekonomi dan Keuangan Syariah di Indonesia.* Jakarta: Bappenas.

Bank Indonesia (BI). (2002) *Blueprint of the Development of Islamic Banking Industry 2002 to 2015.* Jakarta: BI.

Bank Indonesia (BI). (2006) Kebijakan akselerasi pengembangan perbankan Syariah 2007–2008, *BI Presentation Material.* Jakarta: BI.

Bank Negara Malaysia (BNM). (2011) *The BNM Financial Stability and Payment Systems Report 2010.* Kuala Lumpur: BNM.

Bank Negara Malaysia (BNM). (2011a) *Financial Sector Blueprint 2011–2020: Strengthening Our Future.* Kuala Lumpur: BNM.

Baswir, R. (2006) *Mafia Berkeley dan Krisis Ekonomi Indonesia.* Yogyakarta: Pustaka Pelajar.

Chang, J. (2009) Incentives from the Malaysian Government. Paper presented at *Islamic Venture Capital & Private Equity Conference.* Retrieved from: www.assaif.org/content/download/3046/18281/file/Incentives%20from%20the%20Malaysian%20Government-Jennifer%20Chang.pdf

Chapra, M.U. and Khan, T. (2000) *Regulation and Supervision of Islamic Banks. Occasional Paper No. 3.* Jeddah: Islamic Research and Training Institute-Islamic Development Bank (IDB).

Fernando, J.M. (2006) The position of Islam in the constitution of Malaysia, *Journal of Southeast Asian Studies, 37*(2), pp. 249–266.

Financial Services Authority (FSA). (2015) *Roadmap of Indonesian Islamic Banking 2015–2019 (Roadmap Perbankan Syariah Indonesia 2015–2019).* Jakarta: FSA, Republic of Indonesia.

Financial Services Authority (FSA). (2017) *Roadmap of Indonesian Islamic Finance 2015–2019 (Roadmap Keuangan Syariah Indonesia 2015–2019)*. Jakarta: FSA, Republic of Indonesia.

Gomez, E.T. and Jomo, K.S. (1997) *Malaysia's Political Economy: Politics, Patronage and Profits*. Cambridge: Cambridge University Press.

Haneef, M.A. (2001) Islam and economic development in Malaysia – A reappraisal, *Journal of Islamic Studies, 12*(3), pp. 269–290.

Islamic Financial Service Board (IFSB). (2019) *Islamic Financial Services Industry (IFSI) Stability Report 2019*. Kuala Lumpur: IFSB.

Ismal, R. (2011) Islamic banking in Indonesia: Lessons learnt. Paper presented at *Multi-Year Expert Meeting on Services, Development and Trade: The Regulatory and Institutional Dimension*, Geneva, 6–8 April 2011.

Ismal, R. (2013) *Islamic Banking in Indonesia: New Perspectives on Monetary and Financial Issues*. Singapore: John Wiley and Sons.

Krasicka, O. and Nowak, S. (2012) *What's In It For Me? A Primer on Differences Between Islamic and Conventional Finance in Malaysia. IMF Working Paper, No. WP/12/151*. Washington, DC: International Monetary Fund (IMF).

Lai, J. (2012) *Financial Crisis and Institutional Change in East Asia*. Basingstoke, UK: Palgrave Macmillan.

Lai, J. (2015) Industrial policy and Islamic finance, *New Political Economy, 20*(2), pp. 178–198.

Madjid, N. (1987) *Islam, Kemodernan, dan Keindonesiaan*. Bandung: Penerbit Mizan.

Markplus and Bank Indonesia (BI). (2008) *Grand Strategy Developing the Islamic Banking Market*. Jakarta: Directorate of Islamic Banking, BI.

Othman, A., Sari, N.A., Alhabshi, S.O., and Mirakhor, A. (2017). *Macroeconomic Policy and Islamic Finance in Malaysia*. New York: Palgrave Macmillan.

PriceWaterhouseCoopers (PWC) (2006). The 2007 Malaysian Budget, announced on 1 September 2006, provides substantial tax incentives to boost the Islamic finance sector. Retrieved from: www.pwc.com/en_MY/my/assets/publications/ifmsiatax.pdf.

Robison, R. (1990) *Power and Economy in Suharto's Indonesia*. Manila: Journal of Contemporary Asia Publishers.

Wibisono, Y. (2009) Politik ekonomi UU perbankan Syariah peluang dan tantangan regulasi industri perbankan Syariah. *Bisnis dan Birokrasi, Jurnal Ilmu Administrasi dan Organisasi, 16*(2), pp. 105–115.

6 Analysis of financial performance and stability of Asian Islamic banks

1. Introduction

In Chapter 3, we looked at how Indonesia's Islamic banks had suffered from lower profitability, lower efficiency, thinner capital bases, higher cost of funds, and smaller office-branch networks than what conventional banks had achieved. In this chapter, we aim to compare the unique features and performance of Indonesia's Islamic banks with those of Malaysia and Bangladesh.

Çizakça (2011) divides Islamic financing modes into two categories, namely *Shari'ah*-compliant and *Shari'ah*-based financing contracts. Included in the category of *Shari'ah*-compliant mode is a sale-based contract with a predetermined return or mark-up financing, such as *murabaha*, *ijara*, and *salam* contracts, whereas the *Shari'ah*-based mode usually recognizes the genuine profit-and-loss-sharing (PLS) financing which is applied under *mudaraba* and *musharaka* financing contracts. The so-called "*murabaha* syndrome" – a concentration of asset-based financing in the credit portfolio – is widely observed in Islamic banks all over the world. As we discuss later, one of the unique features is that the share of equity-like financing under the *mudaraba/musharaka* contract is relatively high in the credit portfolio of Indonesia's Islamic banks. We discuss whether this feature of being engaged in equity-like financing is related to the low level of Islamic banking penetration in Indonesia.

The rest of this chapter is organized as follows. Section 2 considers why Islamic banks hesitate to engage in equity-like financing. Section 3 compares the performance of Indonesia's Islamic banks with that of Malaysia and Bangladesh to assess their peculiar features. Insofar as the equity-like financing by Indonesian Islamic banks is not considered as "hands-on" financing, the general inefficiency in operations and the seemingly underdeveloped skill in credit risk management are raised as the peculiar features of Indonesia's Islamic banks, compared to the performance of Islamic banks in Malaysia and Bangladesh. Section 4 summarizes the argument in this chapter.

2. Making sense of Islamic banks' conservative credit policy

As discussed in Chapter 4, in the financial restraint framework a bank must pursue and capture the rent (surplus) opportunity to keep its "franchise value" as an incentive, not only for the bank owner to monitor its bank managers, but also to manage its loan portfolio. Under the trust-based *mudaraba* in the PLS mode, the Islamic bank as a lender would be exposed to a more severe information asymmetry in comparison with the asset-backed *murabaha*. Meanwhile, under the equity-like *musharaka* mode of participatory financing, though the bank may be able to monitor the project, the bank as a partner would have to share all the risk and uncertainty exposed to the project. If the Islamic bank rent hypothesis (see Chapter 4, Section 3) is held, the expected return from the *mudaraba* or *musharaka* contract must be high enough to compensate for the risk and uncertainty peculiar to the equity-like financing upon the PLS. In reality, most Islamic banks hesitate to engage in equity-like financing.

How can we make sense of the reality?

First, we should note that if the bank is able to share any loss with the depositor, the bank would be in a neutral position on any project risk and uncertainty under the *mudaraba/musharaka* contract. In reality, the bank faces a "displacement commercial risk" if the rate of return that is distributed to the depositor falls into a lower level than the market rate benchmark (Kasri and Kassim, 2009; Abdul-Rahman et al., 2014). So far as the bank faces difficulty in sharing any loss with the depositor to avoid the displacement commercial risk for maintaining its reputation, the bank would rather not engage in the equity-like financing upon the PLS mode. Second, we should note that the functioning of the PLS mode depends on how well the property rights and tax incentives are structured (Abdul-Rahman et al., 2014). As a crucial point, the existing legal framework in Indonesia is not so protective for the lender's right, which discourages the Islamic banks to engage in a PLS contract. For instance, there exists no specific judicial court reconciling for the case of the default in the PLS contract (Chapra and Khan, 2000).

Third, even if the Islamic bank rent hypothesis is held, the precise calculation of the satisfactory profit margin (the difference between the expected rates of profit received and the rate of profit paid) from the equity-like financing is still difficult under conditions of uncertainty embedded in the mode of PLS. Even mitigating the credit risk by pledging the project asset as collateral is discouraged in the pure mode of PLS. This discourages the bank to engage in equity-like financing. Fourth, in general, equity-like financing is "hands-on" financing. The transaction cost of monitoring the borrower and the project would be higher than the *murabaha* "hands-off" financing.

Considering the above, we should say that unless the existing legal system is altered for reasonably ensuring the lender's right, Islamic banks should not engage in equity-like financing, because engagement under the existing system would not contribute to maintaining their franchise value and reputation or to protecting depositors' funds. However, as mentioned in the introduction to this chapter, one of the unique features of Indonesian Islamic banks is that the share of equity-like financing under the *mudaraba/musharaka* contract is relatively high in their credit portfolio. How can we understand this? To answer the question, let us compare the performance of Indonesia's Islamic banks with that of Malaysia and Bangladesh to clarify their uniqueness.

3. Comparison of Islamic banking sector: Indonesia, Malaysia, and Bangladesh

Let us start with an overview of the Islamic banking sector among three Asian Muslim countries. The banking sector is vital for the economic prosperity of Indonesia, Malaysia, and Bangladesh. In Bangladesh, the size of the banking sector relative to gross domestic product (GDP) was 69.96 per cent in 2010 compared to 32.79 per cent of the stock market (Uddin and Suzuki, 2015, p. 123). Whereas in Malaysia, the size of the banking sector relative to GDP was 303.83 per cent in 2010 compared to 165.85 per cent of the stock market (BNM, 2015). As for Indonesia, using this indicator, the market penetration of the banking sector relative to GDP in 2010 was 44.50 per cent, whereas the size of the stock market was 47.7 per cent (FSA, 2015–2019).[1]

It was in 1983 when the operation of the first Islamic bank began in Bangladesh as well as in Malaysia. Nine years later, the first Indonesian Islamic bank started to operate in 1992. In Indonesia, as of the end of 2015, the number of fully-fledged banks were 12 and the number of conventional banks with Islamic banking windows/branches were 22. In total, 34 banks are engaged in Islamic banking operations. Indonesia's Islamic banking has achieved a share of 5.24 per cent of deposit collections and a 5.21 per cent share of the banking credit market.

Meanwhile, there are 16 Islamic banks in Malaysia which hold an Islamic bank licence from Bank Negara Malaysia (BNM, the central bank). They are composed of five fully-fledged Islamic banks and 11 Islamic subsidiaries of conventional banks (Islamic windows banks). Malaysia's Islamic banking constituted 30.0 per cent of deposit collections and 31.3 per cent of the banking credit market. In Bangladesh, by the end of 2015, there were eight fully-fledged Islamic banks and 16 conventional banks doing Islamic banking by maintaining separate windows. These banks aggregately held 20.43 per cent of deposit collections and a 23.3 per cent share of the banking credit exposure (see Table 6.1).

Table 6.2 shows the return on asset (ROA) and the non-performing loan (NPL) ratios of the Islamic banking sector and the overall banking sector (including the share of Islamic banks) in Indonesia, Malaysia, and Bangladesh during the period from 2007 to 2015. The ROA of the Islamic banking sector of Bangladesh was higher than the overall banking sector in almost all years during the period under study. On the other hand, the NPL ratio of Bangladesh's Islamic banking sector was lower than that of the overall banking sector during the whole period. However, the scenario is entirely reversed in Indonesia's Islamic banks. In both cases, the overall banking sector was performing better than Islamic banks during almost the whole period by presenting a higher ROA and lower NPL

Table 6.1 Comparative position of the Islamic banking sectors in Indonesia, Malaysia, and Bangladesh as of end of December 2015

	Islamic banks	*Banks with dual banking*	*Islamic banking sector*	*Banking sector*
Indonesia				
No. of banks	12 (10.00)	22 (18.33)	34 (28.33)	120
Deposits	174,895 (3.96)	56,280 (1,28)	231,175 (5.24)	4,413,056
Credits/Financing	153,968 (3.76)	59,028 (1.44)	212,996 (5.20)	4,092,104
Malaysia				
No. of banks	5 (9.26)	11 (20.37)	16 (29.63)	54
Deposits	80,410 (4.38)	469,865 (25.62)	550,275 (30.00)	1,834,250
Credits/Financing	61,153 (3.87)	433,853 (27.43)	495,006 (31.30)	1,581,489
Bangladesh				
No. of banks	8 (14.29)	16 (28.57)	24 (42.86)	56
Deposits	1,552.2 (19.32)	89.4 (1.11)	1,641.6 (20.43)	8,033.5
Credits/Financing	1,305.5 (21.93)	81.7 (1.37)	1,387.2 (23.30)	5,952.9

Source: Constructed by the authors based on FSA (2015–2019, 2015a–2019a) as of 31 December 2015, BNM (2015), and the 2015–2016 annual report of Bangladesh Bank.
Note: Amounts are in billion Rupiah (Indonesian currency), million RM (Malaysian currency), and billion BDT (currency of Bangladesh), except for the number of banks. Figures in parentheses represent the percentage of the respective sectors in terms of the banking sector as a whole.

ratio. Meanwhile, in Malaysia, we note that the ROA of the Islamic banking sector is slightly lower in comparison with the banking sector as a whole. In terms of NPLs, we see that the NPL ratio of Islamic banks in Malaysia is more fluctuating and has a slightly lower tendency than that of the banking sector. This suggests that the profitability and stability of Islamic banks vary even among Asian Muslim countries.

We see the different lending patterns of Islamic banks in Indonesia, Malaysia, and Bangladesh in Table 6.3, which displays the income from *murabaha* and equity-like/PLS-based *mudaraba* and *musharaka* during 2008 to 2015. The figures in parentheses in Table 6.3 represent the income from PLS *mudaraba* and *musharaka.* Even though the equity-like financing in Indonesia's Islamic banks created higher contributions in their credit portfolio than in Malaysia and Bangladesh during the period of study, *murabaha* financing obviously still

Table 6.2 The averages of ROA and NPL of Islamic banks in Indonesia, Malaysia, and Bangladesh

Countries/ Years	*2007*	*2008*	*2009*	*2010*	*2011*	*2012*	*2013*	*2014*	*2015*
Indonesia									
ROA (in%)	2.07	1.42	1.48	1.67	1.79	2.14	2.00	0.80	0.84
	(2.78)	(2.33)	(2.60)	(2.86)	(3.03)	(3.11)	(3.08)	(2.85)	(2.32)
NPL (in%)	4.05	3.95	4.01	3.02	2.52	2.22	2.62	4.33	4.4
	(4.07)	(3.20)	(3.31)	(2.56)	(2.17)	(1.87)	(1.77)	(2.16)	(2.49)
Malaysia									
ROA (in%)	1.30	1.00	1.30	1.30	1.00	1.40	1.20	1.10	1.00
	(1.50)	(1.50)	(1.20)	(1.50)	(1.60)	(1.60)	(1.50)	(1.50)	(1.30)
NPL (in%)	3.3	2.3	2.2	2.1	1.6	1.2	1.00	0.90	0.90
	(3.20)	(2.20)	(1.80)	(2.30)	(1.80)	(1.40)	(1.30)	(1.20)	(1.20)
Bangladesh									
ROA (in%)	1.27	1.44	1.67	2.26	1.4	1.62	1.14	1.05	1.07
	(0.90)	(1.20)	(1.40)	(1.80)	(1.50)	(0.60)	(0.90)	(0.60)	(0.80)
NPL (in%)	3.38	2.68	2.17	2.33	2.15	2.98	3.45	3.90	3.81
	(13.20)	(10.80)	(9.20)	(7.30)	(6.10)	(10.00)	(8.90)	(9.70)	(8.80)

Source: Constructed by the authors based on FSA (2015–2019, 2015a–2019a), BNM (2015), and the 2015–2016 annual report of Bangladesh Bank.

Note: Figures in parentheses represent the averages of the banking sector.

placed a dominant financing mode in the Islamic banking operations of these three countries. The so-called *murabaha* syndrome was observed, at least, in Bangladesh's and Malaysia's Islamic banks (it is reported that Malaysia's Islamic banks are dominated by sales-based transactions, especially *murabaha* and *bai bithaman ajil* (deferred sales contracts)).

Indonesian Islamic banks have a relatively higher share of equity-like financing in their credit portfolio. The total equity-like financing exposure has stayed at 27–43 per cent of the total financing in Indonesia's Islamic banks, which is in sharp contrast to the credit portfolio of Bangladesh's and Malaysia's Islamic banks, though that of *murabaha* was always more than 50 per cent during the period 2007–2017 except in 2018, when it was 47 per cent (see Table 6.4). This led us to ask whether the lower profitability and higher NPLs in Indonesia's Islamic banks are related to their credit exposure to equity-like financing.

Here, let us see if there is any difference in the profitability between conventional banking (*riba*-based banking) and Islamic banking in the case of those banks which operate both Islamic and non-Islamic windows/branches simultaneously. We investigated six banks in Indonesia, three banks in Malaysia, and nine banks in Bangladesh. Assuming that both Islamic and non-Islamic windows/branches under the same umbrella are managing almost the same type of risk and uncertainty in banking operations, we compared the ratio of funding cost to income (interest paid/interest received for *riba*-based banking, profit paid/

Table 6.3 Income from ***murabaha*** (as percentage) of different Islamic banks in Indonesia, Malaysia, and Bangladesh

Name of the bank	*Year*							
	2008	*2009*	*2010*	*2011*	*2012*	*2013*	*2014*	*2015*
Indonesia								
PT Bank Syariah Mandiri	47.00	45.00	49.00	58.00	66.00	69.39	69.83	64.29
	(41.00)	(39.00)	(36.00)	(32.00)	(26.00)	(22.95)	(20.11)	(21.01)
PT Bank Muamalat Indonesia	45.00	43.00	43.00	47.00	48.00	46.32	44.66	43.15
	(50.00)	(47.00)	(49.00)	(43.00)	(42.00)	(45.09)	(45.82)	(47.29)
PT Bank Mega Syariah Indonesia	81.00	86.00	88.00	88.00	85.00	89.47	93.40	92.46
	(6.00)	(4.00)	(3.00)	(2.00)	(0.00)	(0.20)	(0.34)	(0.56)
PT Bank Rakyat Indonesia Syariah	87.00	66.00	66.00	59.00	66.00	65.39	65.04	60.27
	(11.00)	(18.00)	(26.00)	(16.00)	(18.00)	(23.04)	(24.39)	(26.48)
PT Bank Negara Indonesia Syariah	NE	NE	51.00	51.00	56.00	64.05	71.58	72.20
			(11.00)	(13.00)	(13.00)	(12.92)	(11.62)	(12.69)
PT Bank Central Asia Syariah	NE	NE	5.00	31.00	36.00	42.99	47.75	48.96
			(9.00)	(14.00)	(27.00)	(50.84)	(46.99)	(45.86)
Malaysia								
Bank Islam Malaysia Berhad	55.26	69.08	59.66	59.66	59.10	46.56	35.61	27.83
	(0.08)	(0.08)	(0.04)	(0.04)	(0.04)	(0.54)	(0.53)	(0.48)
Bank Muamalat Malaysia Berhad	41.57	36.47	40.46	41.67	49.43	57.90	50.14	35.43
	(0.07)	(0.21)	(0.41)	(0.31)	(0.00)	(2.79)	(2.33)	(1.97)
Al Rajhi Banking and Investment Corporation (Malaysia) Berhad	99.88	99.90	99.91	99.90	99.93	99.96	99.96	99.60
	(0.00)	(0.00)	(0.00)	(0.00)	(0.00)	(0.00)	(0.00)	(0.00)
Bangladesh								
Islami Bank Bangladesh Ltd	60.00	54.82	54.25	58.20	58.68	59.18	60.02	58.56
	(1.70)	(2.58)	(3.63)	(4.13)	(3.78)	(4.18)	(2.98)	(2.64)

(*continued*)

Table 6.3 Cont.

Name of the bank	*Year*							
	2008	*2009*	*2010*	*2011*	*2012*	*2013*	*2014*	*2015*
First Security Islami Bank Ltd	77.78 (0.00)	81.36 (0.00)	79.83 (0.00)	75.22 (0.00)	75.22 (0.00)	73.60 (0.00)	75.05 (0.00)	73.31 (0.00)
Export Import Bank of Bangladesh Ltd	22.82 (0.00)	21.48 (0.00)	38.98 (0.00)	42.51 (0.00)	40.09 (0.00)	18.57 (0.66)	16.67 (1.10)	14.01 (1.38)
Shahjalal Islami Bank Ltd	NA	20.32 (0.00)	15.39 (0.00)	15.63 (0.00)	17.10 (0.00)	15.97 (0.05)	11.63 (0.10)	9.44 (0.00)
Social Islami Bank Ltd	NA	20.74 (0.74)	18.41 (0.66)	6.03 (0.42)	4.63 (0.41)	3.49 (0.67)	1.80 (2.26)	1.27 (1.89)
Al-Arafah Islami Bank Ltd	34.74 (0.01)	29.98 (0.01)	35.15 (0.01)	25.66 (0.00)	15.93 (0.00)	11.56 (0.00)	10.75 (0.00)	8.06 (0.00)
Union Bank Ltd	NE	NE	NE	NE	NE	24.16 (0.00)	64.07 (5.75)	63.70 (15.73)

Source: Calculated by the authors based on the annual reports of respective banks.

Note: Figures in parentheses represent the income from PLS mudaraba and musharaka. NA stands for not available. NE stands for not established.

Table 6.4 Composition of ***murabaha*** and PLS, ***mudaraba***, and ***musharaka*** in Indonesian Islamic banks

Type of financing	*Year*											
	2007	*2008*	*2009*	*2010*	*2011*	*2012*	*2013*	*2014*	*2015*	*2016*	*2017*	*2018*
Murabaha	16,553	22,486	26,321	37,508	56,365	88,004	110,565	110,885	115,605	133,956	145,301	151,580
in percentage	59%	59%	56%	55%	55%	60%	60%	59%	58%	57%	53%	47%
Mudaraba and *Musharaka*	9,984	13,616	17,009	23,255	29,189	39,690	53,499	60,466	70,146	86,973	111,081	136,854
in percentage	36%	36%	36%	34%	28%	27%	29%	32%	35%	37%	41%	43%
Others	1,407	2,093	3,556	7,418	17,101	19,811	20,058	15,853	13,691	13,714	16,070	32,242
in percentage	5%	5%	8%	11%	17%	13%	11%	8%	7%	6%	6%	10%
Total financing	27,944	38,195	46,886	68,181	102,655	147,505	184,122	187,204	199,442	234,643	272,452	320,676

Source: Constructed by the authors based on FSA (2015–2019, 2015a–2019a).

profit received for *riba*-free banking) between *riba*-based and *riba*-free (Islamic) banking (Table 6.5). In general, we can see the tendency of the lower ratio of funding cost to income in Islamic banking in comparison with conventional banking.[2]

Next, we compared the ratio of operating expenses to income for all the sample banks (Table 6.6). In Malaysia and Bangladesh, we can see the general tendency of a lower ratio, suggesting higher efficiency in operations in *riba*-free banking than in *riba*-based banking, though the ratio in *riba*-free banking of some Bangladeshi banks does fluctuate. In contrast, the tendency of a lower ratio in *riba*-free banking was not observed in Indonesia. Rather, the ratio was higher and fluctuating, suggesting lower efficiency in operation.

The above tables suggest that while Indonesia's Islamic banks (windows/branches) maintained relatively higher margin spread upon lower funding costs, the lower efficiency in operations may have squeezed their profits. Was the higher cost of operating expenses attributable to the hands-on equity-like financing?

We should note that a large portion of the equity-like financing by Indonesia's Islamic banks is used for a "two-step" financing to their financial subsidiaries or non-bank Islamic financial institutions. This two-step financing is used mainly for channelling to consumer financing demand on the *murabaha* contract. This financing was originally based on the "breakthrough policy" by the regulator, based upon a flexible view in Islamic *fatwa* (opinion) aiming to develop Islamic bank products and to support the development of small and medium enterprises by the stakeholders of Islamic economics associations, i.e. Indonesia Islamic Economist Association and Indonesia Islamic Banking Association (Suzuki et al., 2019). In practice, however, their equity-like *mudaraba/musharaka* financing is construed as a "quasi" *murabaha* by the end users. In our interviews, several directors and managers of Indonesian Islamic banks admitted this practice. In fact, Indonesia's Islamic banks do not expect any higher return from equity-like financing because it is a quasi-*murabaha*.

Indonesia's Islamic banks use *mudaraba/musharaka* financing in construction projects by meeting the working capital demand in the construction period. When the construction is completed, the financing is converted into *murabaha* financing by refinancing the contract between the Islamic bank and the entrepreneur (National *Shari'ah* Board, *Fatwa* No. 89). This type of financing only during the construction period is reported under the category of *mudaraba/musharaka* financing. It is apparent that this type of financing, basically short-term credit, is different from the pure mode of "participatory" equity-like financing (Suzuki et al., 2017).

While the equity-like financing by Indonesia's Islamic banks is not considered as hands-on financing, the general inefficiency in operations (the higher ratio of operating expenses to income) and the seemingly underdeveloped skill in credit risk management (the higher NPL ratio) can be raised as the peculiar features of Indonesia's Islamic banks, compared to the performance of Islamic banks in Malaysia and Bangladesh.

Table 6.5 Cost-to-income ratio in *riba*-based banking[a] and Islamic banking[b] of conventional banks

Name of the bank	*Year*							
	2008	*2009*	*2010*	*2011*	*2012*	*2013*	*2014*	*2015*
Indonesia								
PT Bank BTN	56.24 (35.26)	60.02 (38.05)	48.18 (44.39)	50.79 (48.59)	48.67 (42.79)	49.64 (49.67)	59.02 (56.74)	55.89 (55.40)
PT Bank DKI	51.92 (15.05)	52.29 (19.02)	41.70 (19.82)	40.53 (20.34)	41.81 (12.29)	37.71 (15.24)	40.66 (2856)	39.55 (52.50)
PT Bank Danamon	36.41 (36.77)	33.25 (26.66)	24.73 (16.33)	26.32 (18.01)	23.34 (21.42)	31.86 (21.03)	39.50 (38.03)	38.06 (43.59)
PT Bank BII	44.40 (30.47)	36.77 (33.85)	32.01 (35.39)	35.5 (32.69)	35.08 (19.36)	49.47 (22.37)	55.74 (29.03)	53.87 (21.68)
PT Bank Permata	42.11 (40.28)	46.80 (31.04)	39.86 (18.31)	44.55 (20.27)	47.02 (14.39)	54.91 (20.06)	63.25 (20.37)	59.73 (59.69)
PT Bank BTPN	40.98 (16.68)	41.13 (35.69)	36.02 (27.34)	37.05 (16.33)	34.3 (10.44)	35.59 (10.98)	NA NA	NA NA
Malaysia								
Hong Leong Bank Berhad	55.31 (54.39)	53.83 (53.66)	45.91 (46.51)	49.95 (58.02)	52.19 (55.22)	54.54 (52.79)	52.88 (50.56)	55.10 (57.09)
Affin Bank Berhad	54.33 (58.89)	45.12 (45.51)	50.33 (50.41)	56.85 (55.96)	60.27 (59.12)	58.61 (57.72)	60.61 (58.05)	62.61 (60.67)
CIMB Bank Berhad	49.38 N/A	39.23 (49.77)	38.67 (53.94)	44.92 (55.01)	45.84 (52.48)	45.35 (56.03)	43.32 (54.76)	46.58 (53.35)
Bangladesh								
Prime Bank Ltd	80.29 (65.22)	80.42 (59.84)	64.74 (53.88)	75.76 (64.72)	76.69 (65.98)	84.19 (56.74)	87.08 (62.40)	96.47 (55.81)

(*continued*)

Table 6.5 Cont.

Name of the bank	*Year*							
	2008	*2009*	*2010*	*2011*	*2012*	*2013*	*2014*	*2015*
Bank Asia Ltd	75.18	72.13	65.11	75.59	73.47	79.73	77.08	80.74
	NE	(50.15)	(45.15)	(67.22)	(69.38)	(69.71)	(76.26)	(68.53)
The City Bank Ltd	68.02	63.43	49.27	52.75	61.29	63.53	63.55	65.10
	(57.65)	(81.44)	(81.75)	(104.39)	(73.20)	(79.25)	(73.31)	(50.93)
Dhaka Bank Ltd	71.05	73.58	67.14	76.06	77.90	76.96	78.29	82.74
	(86.78)	(83.45)	(60.07)	(75.20)	(110.93)	(104.15)	(104.63)	(97.18)
Jamuna Bank Ltd	82.30	78.07	72.67	75.25	81.27	89.79	85.73	83.68
	(58.78)	(58.79)	(58.69)	(60.89)	(68.61)	(73.30)	(67.10)	(65.13)
Premier Bank Ltd	75.50	77.30	69.48	77.52	81.09	84.19	80.83	76.79
	(78.97)	(84.95)	(72.43)	(70.31)	(69.18)	(60.42)	(65.64)	(70.01)
Southeast Bank Ltd	84.04	86.55	75.09	86.81	90.11	92.76	86.46	85.25
	(70.30)	(66.97)	(64.32)	(67.85)	(71.95)	(68.97)	(62.04)	(62.95)
AB Bank Ltd	72.49	67.49	61.99	76.21	77.11	77.61	70.20	78.33
	(71.63)	(67.11)	(59.10)	(70.67)	(73.57)	(80.69)	(79.61)	(75.50)
HSBC Bank Ltd	45.37	48.71	40.92	35.51	41.12	51.43	58.82	49.83
	(0.00)	(0.00)	(1.47)	(7.36)	(10.36)	(9.34)	(0.34)	(0.00)

Source: Calculated by the authors based on the annual reports of respective banks.

Notes: Figures in parentheses represent the ratio from Islamic banking operations. NA and NE stand for not available and not established, respectively. PT Bank BII Tbk had been acquired by and converted to PT Bank MayBank Indonesia Tbk based on FSA Decree No.18/KDK.03/2015 dated 23 September 2015.

(a) Cost-to-income ratio in riba-based banking = (interest paid/interest received) ×100.

(b) Cost-to-income ratio in Islamic banking = (profit paid/profit received) ×100.

Table 6.6 Ratio of operating expenses to income in *riba*-based banking[(a)] and Islamic banking[(b)] of conventional banks

Name of the bank	*Year*							
	2008	*2009*	*2010*	*2011*	*2012*	*2013*	*2014*	*2015*
Indonesia								
PT Bank BTN	32.37	31.46	38.36	36.01	38.21	33.09	30.45	29.21
	(36.52)	(47.49)	(52.89)	(5.61)	(31.50)	(17.21)	(17.23)	(18.97)
PT Bank DKI	38.35	43.00	52.96	43.75	45.31	40.45	34.54	34.49
	(86.60)	(54.08)	(73.00)	(43.20)	(83.34)	(22.79)	(29.45)	(59.01)
PT Bank Danamon	47.89	52.33	50.64	50.72	54.65	50.35	44.65	41.50
	(39.18)	(45.71)	(51.44)	(55.25)	(102.12)	(67.37)	(57.21)	(26.88)
PT Bank BII	50.42	64.64	60.91	57.73	53.57	43.68	37.03	34.37
	(40.17)	(49.27)	(111.70)	(24.71)	(31.14)	(13.74)	(35.87)	(26.03)
PT Bank Permata	42.43	37.05	47.99	45.02	47.93	34.52	28.65	28.84
	(24.45)	(29.62)	(41.68)	(54.10)	(68.28)	(4.99)	(10.37)	(27.17)
PT Bank BTPN	36.60	42.68	44.11	39.78	41.16	36.05	NA	NA
	(112.61)	(56.00)	(140.70)	(123.21)	(81.57)	(52.34)	NA	NA
Malaysia								
Hong Leong Bank Berhad	27.86	29.91	31.63	32.21	30.18	33.40	31.72	29.71
	(17.16)	(17.60)	(21.14)	(19.28)	(17.92)	(18.32)	(17.87)	(17.65)
Affin Bank Berhad	33.75	37.77	35.12	29.72	28.78	32.35	40.55	42.83
	(25.42)	(33.77)	(32.77)	(24.22)	(19.51)	(22.64)	(24.59)	(19.98)
CIMB Bank Berhad	36.74	50.70	57.58	50.37	52.80	51.50	46.83	45.79
	NA	(27.98)	(16.68)	(18.86)	(22.28)	(22.32)	(21.76)	(20.12)
Bangladesh								
Prime Bank Ltd	24.77	31.49	33.91	28.12	24.25	28.69	35.98	46.17
	(6.32)	(5.39)	(6.78)	(5.37)	(5.85)	(5.63)	(8.20)	(9.61)

(*continued*)

Table 6.6 Cont.

Name of the bank	*Year*							
	2008	*2009*	*2010*	*2011*	*2012*	*2013*	*2014*	*2015*
Bank Asia Ltd	19.86	24.36	29.79	22.00	21.43	22.77	30.11	33.46
	NE	(50.45)	(18.42)	(12.18)	(9.54)	(11.58)	(16.22)	(17.56)
The City Bank Ltd	38.66	37.85	45.61	39.33	34.75	38.15	43.29	43.30
	(13.58)	(8.57)	(28.29)	(30.48)	(6.40)	(7.33)	(12.31)	(7.10)
Dhaka Bank Ltd	21.08	20.82	24.44	21.21	17.01	18.97	23.46	28.17
	(4.48)	(4.45)	(7.03)	(5.27)	(7.60)	(9.17)	(10.90)	(9.53)
Jamuna Bank Ltd	26.90	29.56	27.86	25.81	23.25	29.44	30.89	35.96
	(11.99)	(9.81)	(9.06)	(9.07)	(6.56)	(6.60)	(9.32)	(10.77)
Premier Bank Ltd	25.04	27.50	42.82	54.43	41.19	40.62	41.16	38.87
	(9.40)	(8.25)	(6.03)	(3.30)	(3.29)	(3.17)	(3.70)	(5.34)
Southeast Bank Ltd	15.40	15.68	19.00	16.87	15.22	17.79	19.74	23.04
	(8.56)	(7.80)	(8.31)	(6.85)	(5.32)	(5.26)	(5.57)	(5.88)
AB Bank Ltd	26.91	29.40	36.57	28.54	27.71	26.20	25.55	27.79
	(3.64)	(3.56)	(6.50)	(4.02)	(3.33)	(3.78)	(5.22)	(6.79)
HSBC Bank Ltd	23.40	28.04	31.72	32.84	27.68	38.95	42.80	61.63
	(9.32)	(6.56)	(2,247.27)	(39.23)	(15.38)	(14.45)	(0.00)	(0.00)

Source: Calculated by the authors based on the annual reports of respective banks.

Notes: Figures in parentheses represent the ratio from Islamic banking operations. NA and NE stand for not available and not established, respectively. PT Bank BII Tbk had been acquired by and converted to PT Bank MayBank Indonesia Tbk. by FSA Decree No.18/KDK.03/2015 dated 23 September 2015.

(a) Ratio of operating expenses to income in riba-based banking = (interest paid/interest received) ×100.

(b) Ratio of operating expenses to income in Islamic banking of conventional banks = (profit paid/profit received) ×100.

4. Summary

Compared to conventional banks, Indonesia's Islamic banks suffer from lower profitability, lower efficiency, thinner capital bases, higher cost of funds, and smaller office-branch networks. Is this phenomenon generally observed in other Muslim countries? In this chapter, we find that this phenomenon – especially lower profitability, lower efficiency, and less stability – is rather peculiar to the case of Indonesia. The higher ratio of operating expenses to income is not attributable to the exposure of hands-on equity-like financing, because the nature of the *musharaka* financing adopted by Indonesia's Islamic banks is not a type of purely participatory financing. Despite this, general inefficiency in operations and seemingly underdeveloped skills in credit risk management in Indonesian Islamic banks are observed. This phenomenon should be critically assessed.

Notes

1 This condition does not change significantly when we find that market penetration in the banking sector relative to GDP was 55.7 per cent as of 31 December 2015, whereas the size of the stock market was 42.2 per cent (FSA, 2015–2019; BPS, 2016). This suggests that the overall financial deepening level in Indonesia is low. As mentioned in Chapter 4, Section 4, this is another big "puzzle" for the Indonesian economy.

2 In Chapter 3, we suggested a higher cost of funds of Indonesia's Islamic banks in comparison with conventional banks. It appears that the observation in Table 6.5 is not consistent with our analysis in Chapter 3. One hypothesis is that the funding cost under the same umbrella (Islamic windows/branches) is lower than that of fully-fledged Islamic banks. This entails further investigation.

References

Abdul-Rahman, A., Latif, R.A., and Abdullah, M.A. (2014) Failure and potential of profit-loss sharing contracts: A perspective of New Institutional Economic (NIE) theory, *Pacific-Basin Finance Journal*, *28*, pp. 136–151.

Badan Pusat Statistik (BPS) (2016). *Produk Domestik Bruto Indonesia Menurut Pengeluaran 2011–2015*. Jakarta: BPS.

Bank Negara Malaysia (BNM). (2015) *The BNM Financial Stability and Payment Systems Report 2014*. Kuala Lumpur: BNM.

Chapra, M.U. and Khan, T. (2000) *Regulation and Supervision of Islamic Banks. Occasional Paper No. 3*. Jeddah: Islamic Research and Training Institute-Islamic Development Bank (IDB).

Çizakça, M. (2011) *Islamic Capitalism and Finance: Origins, Evolution and the Future*. Cheltenham, UK: Edward Elgar.

Financial Services Authority (FSA). (2015–2019) *Indonesian Banking Statistics December 2014–2018*. Jakarta: FSA, Republic of Indonesia.

Financial Services Authority (FSA). (2015a–2019a) *Indonesian Islamic Banking Statistics December 2014–2018*. Jakarta: FSA, Republic of Indonesia.

Kasri, R.A. and Kassim S.H. (2009) Empirical determinants of saving in the Islamic banks: Evidence from Indonesia, *Islamic Economics*, *22*(2), pp. 3–23.

Suzuki, Y., Uddin, S.M.S., Pramono, S. (2019) Do Islamic banks need to earn extra profits? A comparative analysis on banking sector rent in Bangladesh and Indonesia, *Journal of Islamic Accounting and Business Research*, *10*(3), pp. 369–381. doi: https://doi.org/10.1108/JIABR-01-2017-0003

Suzuki, Y., Uddin, S.M.S., Pramono, S., and Khan, S. (2017) Islamic bank rent: Comparison among Bangladesh, Indonesia, Malaysia, and Pakistan, in Y. Suzuki, M.D. Miah, M.K. Wanniarachchige, and S.M.S. Uddin (Eds) *Banking and Economic Rent in Asia: Rent Effects, Financial Fragility, and Economic Development*. Abingdon, UK: Routledge, pp. 121–137.

Uddin, S.M.S. and Suzuki, Y. (2015) The dynamics of concentration and competition in the banking sector of Bangladesh: An empirical investigation, *South Asian Journal of Management*, *22*(1), pp. 114–136.

7 Analysis of the dynamic concentration and competition levels of the Islamic banking sector in Indonesia

1. Introduction

In Chapter 3, we pointed out that Islamic banks were exposed to more severe competition than conventional banks in the market of asset-based consumer financing in, for instance, the automotive business. Since there was no differentiation between the financing products for automobiles/motorcycles, it was extremely difficult for Islamic banks to simply apply "mark-up" pricing to compete with conventional banks in the segment. We assumed that the higher cost of funds in Islamic banks may have squeezed their profit margins.

This chapter aims to analyse Indonesia's credit market structure, concentration over time, and competition configuration to clarify how Indonesian Islamic banks face stiffer competition with conventional banks, as well as among themselves, in the banking industry.

The rest of this chapter is organized into three further sections. Section 2 gives an overview of the debate about the correlation between banking market competition and bank efficiency. We argue that although there is no clear-cut mechanism to determine the correlation between competition and efficiency in the banking sector, the case of Indonesia's Islamic banks would support the competition-inefficiency hypothesis.

Section 3 attempts to trace the changes in the concentration level in the overall banking sector as well as that among Islamic banks. We argue that the two-fold unfavourable conditions experienced by Islamic banks have been the reason for their lag in capability and competency, and worsening profitability performances have become the catalysts for lower levels of efficiency and performance in Indonesian Islamic banks. Section 4 gives our concluding comments.

2. Debate over market competition and efficiency

The debate over the impact of the banking market structure on profitability and financial stability has controversially been between two paradigms. One hypothesis insists on the positive impact of the concentration in the banking segment. Beck et al. (2006) argue that a concentrated banking market would contribute to the stability and resilience of the banking industry to respond to potential financial turmoil. A study conducted by Mirzaei et al. (2011) demonstrates that market power has a significant impact on a bank's profitability in advanced economies (although they point out that it has no significant impact in developing economies). The other hypothesis doubts the positive impact. For instance, Calem and Carlino (1991) point out that the less-concentrated banking market structure creates a higher level of efficiency in banking and is less prone to potential financial crises. Abbasoglu et al. (2007) argue that a concentrated market may increase the revenue for the banks, but it is not beneficial for the banks' customers.

The issue of banking stability and solvency is an important macroeconomic issue for the "overall" banking industry. In this book, we are mainly concerned about the relatively lower profitability and lower efficiency of Indonesia's Islamic banks in comparison with conventional banks. Therefore, we focus on the debate over the relationship between banks' competitive levels and efficiency. In general, the theories about the correlation of competition and efficiency are categorized into two hypotheses, namely the competition-efficiency hypothesis and the competition-inefficiency hypothesis (Sastrosuwito, 2012).

The basic arguments for the competition-efficiency hypothesis are constructed on the "quiet life hypothesis" proposition suggested by Hicks (1935), which states that the monopolistic market power tends to deteriorate general efficiency as the bank managers relish the comfort zone of the lesser competitive market (Casu and Girardone, 2008; Sastrosuwito, 2012). Weill (2004) describes the mechanism of the "welfare effect" in the competitive market as the source of efficiency. The created conditions under the competitive market push the banks to lower the offering lending rate; thus, the market provides the incentives for the banks to engage in the minimum cost of operations to improve the efficiency in the long run.

There are several empirical studies which are in line with the competition-efficiency hypothesis. For instance, Wanniarachchige and Suzuki (2010) suggest that the increased competition in the Sri Lankan banking industry in the period of 2003 to 2007 resulted in higher efficiency of the banking system, which successfully managed technological and managerial improvement. Sastrosuwito (2012) shows that the increased competition in the Indonesian banking sector after the period of political oppression had a positive impact on the efficiency of the banking sector. These empirical studies support the argument of the competition-efficiency hypothesis as the policy to increase competitive levels in improving efficiency.

On the other hand, the competition-inefficiency hypothesis argues that the increasing climate of competition leads to general inefficiency in the banking industry. Sastrosuwito (2012) underlines the rationale behind this hypothesis as a tendency of less stable and shorter relationships between the bank and the customers. This argument can be held under the competitive market of the banking industry in two ways: firstly, the inefficiency is the result of a higher probability of customers moving to alternative banks due to better prices offered (Chan et al., 1986; Boot and Schmeits, 2005; Sastrosuwito, 2012). Secondly, it is the result of the loss of information by the banks about their customers because of the short-term relationship. Consequently, the banks must bear a higher cost of information to maintain their existing customers and attract new customers. The competition-inefficiency hypothesis underlines the issue of asymmetric information and transaction costs of screening and monitoring in the relationship between the bank and the client.

From the financial restraint paradigm discussed in Chapter 4, we can argue that the increased competition would lead to decreased rent opportunities, resulting in the decline in franchise value owing partly to the potential moral hazard behaviour. Hellmann et al. (1997) opine that if the deposit rate is freely determined in the market, it would create the incentives for banks to increase their deposit rates for expanding their deposit base with a compromise on eroding profits, diminishing franchise value by increasing risk-taking behaviour. Keeley (1990) explains how, in referring to the case of the United States, severe competition decreases rent opportunities and lessens the incentive for the banks to conduct prudent banking practices.

There are also several empirical studies which support the hypothesis. Kumbhakar et al. (2001) prove that the increased competition in the Spanish market as a result of its banking regulatory reforms caused a deterioration of bank efficiency, mainly because of over-expansion under the excess competition. Uddin and Suzuki (2014) investigated the impact of competition levels in Bangladeshi banks on bank performance, focusing on return on assets and bank efficiency indicators. They show that the increased competition level in the banking industry had a negative correlation with bank profitability and efficiency. This study underlines the necessity for regulatory reforms to ensure the necessary incentives for banks to improve their performance even within a competitive environment.

There are studies suggestive of the correlation between competition and efficiency related to Islamic banking. Ariss (2010) explored the significance of the competitive condition on bank profitability in conventional and Islamic banks in 13 countries over the period between 2000 and 2006. This study finds that for the conventional banks, market power increases profitability. However, for the Islamic banks, the correlation is not proven. Mirzaei (2012) examined the effects of market power on the stability and performance of Islamic and conventional banks in 12 Islamic countries in the Middle East over the period between 1999 and 2008. Mirzaei shows that for the Islamic banks, the market concentration had no significant impact on their profitability and stability.

There is no clear-cut mechanism to determine the correlation between competition and efficiency in the banking sector. Therefore, the accumulation of empirical studies is important to clarify under what conditions the competition-inefficient (or efficient) hypothesis would be held. As we discussed in Chapters 3 and 4, we assume that the lower profitability and efficiency of Indonesian Islamic banks is attributable to the stiffer competition with conventional banks under the neoliberal regulatory framework, if the Islamic bank rent hypothesis is held. In our view, the case of Indonesia's Islamic banks would support the competition-inefficiency hypothesis.

3. Concentration and efficiency

This section aims to examine the market concentration and competition levels in the banking segment surrounding Indonesia's Islamic banks by applying two concentration measurement methods: the k-bank concentration ratio and the Herfindahl-Hirschman index (HHI).

The k*-bank concentration ratio*

This method is well-known and is widely used to measure the market concentration upon the merit of its simplicity (Meilak, 2008; Uddin and Suzuki, 2015). The ratio is calculated by summing the market shares of the largest banks in the industry in the investigated periods. Symbolically, it can be formulated as follows:

$$CR_k = \sum_{i=1}^{n} S_i$$

Where S_i is the market share for a particular bank(s) and k is the number of the largest banks in the industry. Determining the value of k is basically at the examiner's discretion. The k-bank concentration ratio ranges between zero and one (Tushaj, 2010; Suzuki and Uddin, 2014).

The Herfindahl-Hirschman index (HHI)

In adopting the HHI, if we consider that the bank market concentration should be measured by weight, greater weights should be attributed to the larger banks (Tushaj, 2010; Uddin and Suzuki, 2015). In calculating this index, the market share of each bank is squared and summed in each period. The HHI is defined as follows:

$$HHI = \sum_{i=1}^{n} S_i^2$$

Where S_i is the market share of bank i and n is the number of banks in the industry. Based on this formula, the index range is $(1/n) < \text{HHI} < 1$, meaning that the maximum concentration in the unity is attained in a monopoly market, whereas the minimum concentration $(1/n)$ happens when each bank has an equal market share in the industry.

4. Analysis and empirical results

Here, we measure the k-bank concentration ratios of the top three/five banks to examine the concentration level of Indonesia's banking industry in terms of the total assets, credit/financing, and deposits during the period between 2006 and 2018 (Table 7.1).

Table 7.1 Concentration ratio based on total assets, total credit, and total deposits of the Indonesian banking industry

Based on total assets	*2006*	*2007*	*2008*	*2009*	*2010*	*2011*	*2012*	*2013*	*2014*	*2015*	*2016*	*2017*	*2018*
CR-*k*3	0.36	0.37	0.37	0.39	0.39	0.38	0.38	0.37	0.39	0.39	0.40	0.41	0.41
CR-*k*5	0.50	0.51	0.50	0.52	0.52	0.51	0.51	0.50	0.51	0.51	0.53	0.54	0.55
Based on total credit	*2006*	*2007*	*2008*	*2009*	*2010*	*2011*	*2012*	*2013*	*2014*	*2015*	*2016*	*2017*	*2018*
CR-*k*3	0.31	0.31	0.33	0.35	0.35	0.35	0.36	0.36	0.36	0.37	0.38	0.39	0.39
CR-*k*5	0.44	0.44	0.46	0.48	0.48	0.47	0.48	0.48	0.48	0.49	0.51	0.52	0.53
Based on total deposits	*2006*	*2007*	*2008*	*2009*	*2010*	*2011*	*2012*	*2013*	*2014*	*2015*	*2016*	*2017*	*2018*
CR-*k*3	0.38	0.40	0.40	0.42	0.41	0.39	0.39	0.39	0.40	0.40	0.41	0.41	0.42
CR-*k*5	0.52	0.53	0.54	0.56	0.54	0.52	0.52	0.51	0.52	0.52	0.54	0.54	0.56

Source: Annual reports of each bank for the period 2006–2018 and FSA (2015–2019), constructed by the authors.

We note that, in the market structure of the Indonesian banking industry, the six biggest banks comprising of state-owned banks and fully private conglomerate banks were dominant during the period. In fact, among not less than 100 commercial banks in Indonesia, the top three banks held around 36 to 41 per cent of the total assets, 31 to 39 per cent of the total credit, and 38 to 42 per cent of the total deposits in the banking industry. The top five banks controlled around 50 to 55 per cent of the total assets, 44 to 53 per cent of the total credit, and 52 to 56 per cent of the total deposits. The *k*-bank concentration ratios during the period between 2006 and 2018 suggest that there was no significant change in the competition/concentration levels of the banking industry in Indonesia and around half of the market share was occupied by the top five banks.

This high concentration of controlling financial assets in the banking sector raises a concern related to the issue of financial inclusion in Indonesia. The composition of the number of deposit accounts and the deposit amount in each segment reported by the Indonesia Deposit Insurance Corporation (IDIC) (2018) suggests the occurrence of an "oligarchic financial resource grip" in the Indonesian deposit market. Figure 7.1 shows the number of deposit accounts and the total deposit amount in each segment as of the end of 2018. Apparently, the depositors in the richest segment held almost half of the total deposit amount, even though the number of deposit accounts held by them was quite marginal, less than 0.1 per cent. This structure may be reflected in each bank's strategy of deposit-taking. The top five or six banks may have enclosed the depositors in the richest segment.

Next, we look at the concentration levels in Indonesia's Islamic banking industry during the period of 2004 to 2018. We classify the entire population of fully-fledged Islamic banks and Islamic bank business divisions/windows into four categories: state/district-owned Islamic banks (IB-SDO), privately owned

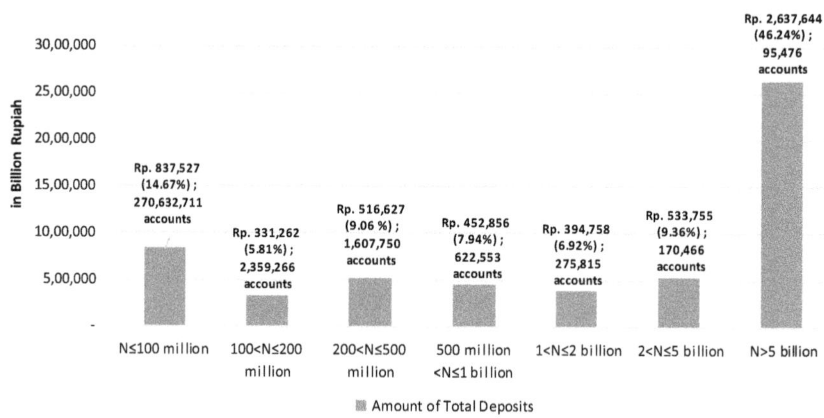

Figure 7.1 Composition of deposit accounts and the total amount in each category in Indonesian banks as of 31 December 2018.

Source: IDIC (2018), constructed by the authors.

Islamic banks (IB-PO), state/district-owned Islamic bank windows (IBW-SDO), and privately owned Islamic bank windows (IBW-PO). The main players of fully-fledged Islamic banks owned by the state (as the subsidiaries of state-owned conventional banks) in Indonesia are: PT Bank Syariah Mandiri (BSM), PT Bank Rakyat Indonesia Syariah (BRIS), and PT Bank Negara Indonesia Syariah (BNIS). These Islamic banks are under each holding company, which is also the main player in conventional banking in Indonesia. The category of Islamic banks owned by the private sector is dominated by PT Bank Muamalat Indonesia (BMI), which was established as the first Indonesian Islamic bank and recognized as the pioneer in Islamic banking in Indonesia.

The share of each category of the total assets, third-party funds/deposits, and financing in Indonesia is shown in Tables 7.2, 7.3, and 7.4, respectively.

During the period from 2004 to 2018, Indonesia's Islamic banking was dominated by Islamic banks owned by the state/district government (keeping around 36 to 49 per cent of the total assets) and Islamic banks owned by private companies (keeping around 21 to 40 per cent of the total assets). In other words, the presence of Islamic bank windows was limited in Indonesia. The

Table 7.2 Total assets of Islamic banks and Islamic bank windows during the period 2004–2018

Year	*Total assets*							
	Amount (in million Rupiah)				*Percentage*			
	IB-SDO	*IB-PO*	*IBW-SDO*	*IBW-PO*	*IB-SDO*	*IB-PO*	*IBW-SDO*	*IBW-PO*
2004	6,869,949	5,610,675	1,878,846	371,155	47%	38%	13%	3%
2005	8,272,965	8,323,956	2,851,475	1,431,453	40%	40%	14%	7%
2006	9,554,967	10,715,534	4,238,426	2,213,103	36%	40%	16%	8%
2007	13,146,607	13,140,465	6,634,190	3,605,361	36%	36%	18%	10%
2008	18,532,699	16,313,109	9,157,931	5,059,375	38%	33%	19%	10%
2009	25,214,921	22,545,766	12,445,544	6,471,540	38%	34%	19%	10%
2010	47,663,652	31,312,970	8,976,544	8,958,004	49%	32%	9%	9%
2011	71,189,111	45,343,160	13,565,742	15,042,922	49%	31%	9%	10%
2012	83,203,072	63,378,876	19,117,909	27,710,651	43%	33%	10%	14%
2013	100,769,867	77,606,114	25,573,431	36,006,245	42%	32%	11%	15%
2014	112,882,304	91,488,112	28,427,865	39,151,907	42%	34%	10%	14%
2015	124,057,922	88,330,712	33,048,210	49,798,215	42%	30%	11%	17%
2016	161,033,754	92,868,946	40,832,299	60,896,433	45%	26%	11%	17%
2017	184,605,968	102,923,316	52,626,266	84,237,238	43%	24%	12%	20%
2018	214,180,455	101,554,053	60,159,201	100,512,160	45%	21%	13%	21%

Source: Annual reports of each bank for the period 2004–2018 and FSA (2015–2019), constructed by the authors.

Notes:
IB-SDO: Islamic banks – state district owned
IB-PO: Islamic banks – privately owned
IBW-SDO: Islamic bank windows – state district owned
IBW-PO: Islamic bank windows – privately owned

Table 7.3 Total third-party funds/deposits of Islamic banks and Islamic bank windows during the period 2004–2018

Year	*Total deposits*							
	Amount (in million Rupiah)				*Percentage*			
	IB-SDO	*IB-PO*	*IBW-SDO*	*IBW-PO*	*IB-SDO*	*IB-PO*	*IBW-SDO*	*IBW-PO*
2004	5,725,007	4,610,300	1,038,801	182,626	50%	40%	9%	2%
2005	7,037,506	6,572,152	1,347,756	833,821	45%	42%	9%	5%
2006	8,219,267	8,994,984	2,110,639	2,220,733	38%	42%	10%	10%
2007	11,230,705	10,860,783	1,156,172	2,225,557	44%	43%	5%	9%
2008	15,434,387	12,915,082	5,277,386	3,467,714	42%	35%	14%	9%
2009	21,148,060	18,540,681	8,379,253	4,830,502	40%	35%	16%	9%
2010	40,579,083	24,444,831	5,409,363	6,287,749	53%	32%	7%	8%
2011	61,494,871	36,090,984	8,665,583	10,831,823	53%	31%	7%	9%
2012	71,667,383	48,705,806	11,581,670	18,118,165	48%	32%	8%	12%
2013	85,380,484	59,364,641	15,705,075	24,660,151	46%	32%	8%	13%
2014	98,014,701	73,379,711	19,572,811	27,922,391	45%	34%	9%	13%
2015	106,364,006	73,021,002	24,439,038	32,025,382	45%	31%	10%	14%
2016	136,554,687	70,687,757	30,647,604	40,625,886	49%	25%	11%	15%
2017	158,272,609	80,168,554	37,521,556	58,973,151	47%	24%	11%	18%
2018	180,322,477	77,418,351	42,256,337	71,965,319	48%	21%	11%	19%

Source: Annual reports of each bank for the period 2004–2018 and FSA (2015–2019), constructed by the authors.

Notes:
IB-SDO: Islamic banks – state district owned
IB-PO: Islamic banks – privately owned
IBW-SDO: Islamic bank windows – state district owned
IBW-PO: Islamic bank windows – privately owned

share of IBW-SDO stayed in the range of around 9 to 19 per cent, while the share of IBW-PO stayed in the range of 3 to 21 per cent (in passing, we should note that during the last eight years, IBW-PO recorded a higher share than IBW-SDO). This is in sharp contrast with the market structure of Malaysia's Islamic banking, where the Islamic bank windows/subsidiaries of the conventional banks are dominant, rather than their fully-fledged Islamic bank counterparts. For instance, the Islamic bank windows/subsidiaries of the conventional banks held around 80 per cent of the market share in the Islamic banking industry in 2015 (Ariff, 2017).

Figure 7.2 presents the Islamic bank concentration index using the HHI based on the total assets, deposits (third-party funds), and financing of Indonesian Islamic banks during the period of 2004 to 2018.

We see that during the period of 2004 to 2018, the market concentration of Islamic banks based on the total assets, deposits, and financing had a declining trend. Apparently, the level of competition among Islamic banks in Indonesia had intensified during the period from 2004 to 2018, especially since 2010. In our

Table 7.4 Total financing of Islamic banks and Islamic bank windows during the period 2004–2018

Year	*Total financing*							
	Amount (in million Rupiah)				*Percentage*			
	IB-SDO	*IB-PO*	*IBW-SDO*	*IBW-PO*	*IB-SDO*	*IB-PO*	*IBW-SDO*	*IBW-PO*
2004	5,209,757	4,359,197	1,178,546	401,291	47%	39%	11%	4%
2005	5,720,912	6,520,342	1,876,546	1,114,142	38%	43%	12%	7%
2006	7,153,908	8,775,789	2,687,459	1,995,850	35%	43%	13%	10%
2007	10,112,645	10,460,938	4,595,263	2,026,219	37%	38%	17%	7%
2008	16,683,331	12,777,735	6,700,119	3,360,419	42%	32%	17%	9%
2009	24,133,267	15,904,999	3,461,515	3,386,657	51%	34%	7%	7%
2010	34,989,469	21,653,184	6,393,683	4,209,195	52%	32%	10%	6%
2011	53,355,934	31,056,415	8,856,687	6,658,262	53%	31%	9%	7%
2012	66,750,289	45,676,206	19,997,814	15,080,819	45%	31%	14%	10%
2013	79,399,502	58,548,170	19,365,381	17,980,766	45%	33%	11%	10%
2014	84,349,699	64,315,045	22,098,927	28,912,986	42%	32%	11%	14%
2015	90,357,180	64,126,916	25,977,405	34,696,348	42%	30%	12%	16%
2016	111,734,131	66,506,448	28,758,469	45,157,487	44%	26%	11%	18%
2017	121,485,177	68,997,627	35,907,633	61,701,588	42%	24%	12%	21%
2018	140,676,428	62,598,911	43,222,830	76,233,340	44%	19%	13%	24%

Source: Annual reports of each bank for the period 2004–2018 and FSA (2015–2019), constructed by the authors.

Notes:
IB-SDO: Islamic banks – state district owned
IB-PO: Islamic banks – privately owned
IBW-SDO: Islamic bank windows – state district owned
IBW-PO: Islamic bank windows – privately owned

view, this is consistent with the competition-inefficiency hypothesis in explaining the slow-paced growth of Indonesia's Islamic banking.

Going back to the measurements of *k*-bank concentration ratios, suggesting that the dominance by the big three or five commercial banks has remained unchanged, the results imply that the entry barrier for Islamic banks to compete with the big commercial banks was set very high, especially in the consumer financing segment. Meanwhile, the competition level among Islamic banks intensified during the mentioned period.

According to our interview with a senior banker at an Indonesian Islamic bank, most Islamic banks actually focus on retail banking (consumer financing). The banker admitted that it was very difficult to compete with large conventional banks due to the thin capital base, the lack of capacity and experience of being engaged in corporate finance, and the higher cost of funds. In addition, the banker admitted that there was more severe competition in the retail and consumer finance sector. The competition among Islamic banks has been intensified, too. The comments from the banker endorse our interpretation of

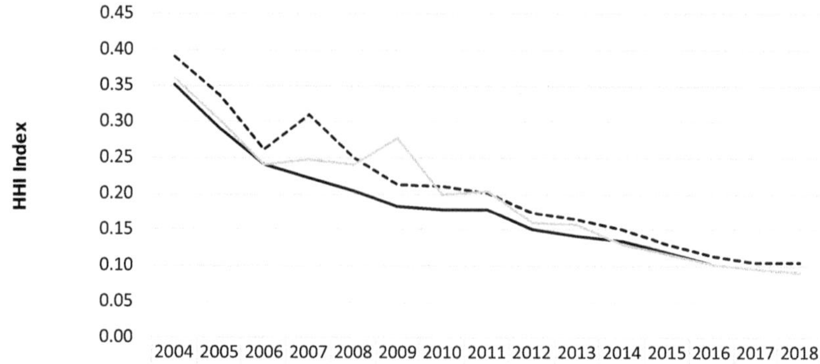

	2004	2005	2006	2007	2008	2009	2010	2011	2012	2013	2014	2015	2016	2017	2018
Total Assets	0.35	0.29	0.24	0.22	0.20	0.18	0.18	0.18	0.15	0.14	0.13	0.12	0.10	0.09	0.09
Total Deposits	0.39	0.34	0.26	0.31	0.25	0.21	0.21	0.20	0.17	0.16	0.15	0.13	0.11	0.11	0.10
Total Financing	0.36	0.30	0.24	0.25	0.24	0.28	0.20	0.20	0.16	0.16	0.13	0.12	0.10	0.10	0.09

Total Assets ----- Total Deposits Total Financing

Figure 7.2 HHI concentration based on total assets, total deposits, and total financing of Islamic banks in Indonesia for the period 2004–2018.

Source: Annual report of each bank and FSA (2015–2019), constructed by the authors.

the results from analysing the concentration levels in the banking industry in Indonesia.

5. Concluding comments

This chapter aimed to analyse the Indonesian banking market structure, concentration over time, and competition configuration to clarify how Indonesia's Islamic banks were facing stiffer competition with conventional banks, as well as between each other, in the banking industry. We point out that two unfavourable conditions – the dominant presence of the big three or five commercial banks in the banking sector and the intensified competition among Islamic banks, especially since 2010 – experienced by Islamic banks have been the reason for their lag in capability and competency; and worsening profitability performances have become the catalysts for the lower levels of efficiency and performance in Indonesia's Islamic banks. There is no clear-cut mechanism to determine the correlation between competition and efficiency in the banking sector. In our view, the case of Indonesia's Islamic banks would support the competition-inefficiency hypothesis. Having acknowledged that the level of financial deepening in Indonesia is relatively low compared to the other developing countries, we should note that the Indonesian banking sector has not yet fully functioned as an engine of economic growth. In our assessment, the concentration level of the banking industry in the period 2006–2018 shows that almost half of the financial assets in the banking sector were held by the top five banks. As long as the depositors in the richest segment are enclosed by them, it is difficult for Islamic banks as newcomers to penetrate the segment for contributing to their efficient funding.

We may say that Islamic banks should explore a different domain to capitalize on their own advantages, for instance, utilizing equity-like financing such as the ***musharaka*** contract for small- and medium-sized enterprises. However, the equity-like mode of financing is associated with higher risks for the banks. This is a dilemma faced by the Islamic banking industry in Indonesia. Under the current regulatory framework, it seems that the Islamic bankers are losing their incentives to challenge the dilemma.

References

Abbasoglu, O.F., Aysan, A.F., and Gunes, A. (2007) Concentration, competition, efficiency and profitability of the Turkish banking system in the post-crises period, *MPRA Paper No. 5494*. Retrieved from: www.econ.boun.edu.tr/content/wp/ISS_EC_07_20.pdf

Ariff, M. (2017) Islamic banking in Malaysia: The changing landscape, *Institutions and Economies*, *9*(2), pp. 1–13.

Ariss, R.T. (2010) Competitive conditions in Islamic and conventional banking: A global perspective, *Review of Financial Economics*, *19*(10), pp. 101–108.

Beck, T., Demirguc-Kunt, A., and Levine, R. (2006) Bank concentration, competition and crisis: First results, *Journal of Banking and Finance*, *30*, pp. 1581–1603.

Boot, A.W. and Schmeits, A. (2005) The competitive challenge in banking, *Amsterdam Center for Law and Economics Working Paper No. 2005–08*. Retrieved from: http://ssrn.com/paper=841285

Calem, P.S. and Carlino, G.A. (1991) The concentration/conduct relationship in bank deposit market, *The Review of Economics and Statistics*, *73*(2), pp. 268–276.

Casu, B. and Girardone, C. (2008) Integration and efficiency in EU banking markets, Essex Finance Centre Discussion Paper No. 08/01, Chapters in SUERF Studies, pp. 89–110.

Chan, Y., Greenbaum, S.I., and Thakor, A.V. (1986) Information reusability, competition and bank assets quality, *Journal of Banking and Finance*, *10*(2), pp. 255–276.

Financial Services Authority (FSA). (2015–2019) *Indonesian Islamic Banking Statistics December 2014–2018*. Jakarta: FSA, Republic of Indonesia.

Hellmann, T., Murdock, K., and Stiglitz, J. (1997) Financial restraint: Toward a new paradigm, in M. Aoki, H.-K. Kim, and M. Okuno-Fujiwara (Eds) *The Role of Government in East Asian Economic Development: Comparative Institutional Analysis*. Oxford: Clarendon Press, pp. 163–207.

Hicks, J.R. (1935) Annual survey of economic theory: The theory of monopoly, *Econometrica*, *3*(1), pp. 1–20.

Indonesia Deposit Insurance Corporation (IDIC). (2018) *Distribusi Simpanan Bank Umum Periode Desember 2018*. Jakarta: IDIC.

Keeley, M.C. (1990) Deposit insurance, risk, and market power in banking, *The American Economic Review*, *80*(5), pp. 1183–1200.

Kumbhakar, S.C., Lozano-Vivas, A., Lovell, C.A.K., and Iftekhar, H. (2001) The effects of deregulation on the performance of financial institutions: The case of Spanish savings banks, *Journal of Money, Credit, and Banking*, *33*(1), pp. 101–120.

Meilak, C. (2008) Measuring export concentration: The implication for small states, *Bank of Valletta Review*, *37*, pp. 35–48.

Mirzaei, A. (2012) The effect of market power on stability and performance of Islamic and conventional banks, *Islamic Economic Studies*, *18*(1 and 2), pp. 45–81.

Mirzaei, A., Guy Liu, G., and Moore, T. (2011) Does market structure matter on banks' profitability and stability? Emerging versus advanced economies. *Economics and Finance Working Paper Series, Working Paper No. 11–12*, Brunel University, UK. Retrieved from: www.brunel.ac.uk/_data/assets/pdf_file/0006/127482/1112.pdf

Sastrosuwito, S. (2012) Determinants and impact of bank efficiency on economic growth: Empirical evidence from Indonesia. Unpublished PhD dissertation, Ritsumeikan Asia Pacific University, Japan.

Suzuki, Y. and Uddin, S.M.S. (2014) Islamic bank rent: A case study of Islamic banking in Bangladesh, *International Journal of Islamic and Middle Eastern Finance and Management*, *7*(2), pp. 170–181.

Tushaj, A. (2010) Market concentration in the banking sector: Evidence from Albania, *Working paper No. 73*. Bamberg Economic Research Group on Government and Growth, Bamberg University, Germany. Retrieved from: www.econstor.eu/bitstream/10419/38826/1/625730917.pdf

Uddin, S.M.S. and Suzuki, Y. (2014) The impact of competition on bank performance in Bangladesh: An empirical study, *International Journal of Financial Services Management*, *7*(1), pp. 73–94.

Uddin, S.M.S. and Suzuki, Y. (2015) The dynamics of concentration and competition in the banking sector of Bangladesh: An empirical investigation, *South Asian Journal of Management*, *22*(1), pp. 114–136.

Wanniarachchige, M.K. and Suzuki, Y. (2010) Bank competition and efficiency: The case of Sri Lanka, *Asia Pasific World*, *1*(1), pp. 117–131.

Weill, L. (2004) On the relationship between competition and efficiency in the EU banking sectors, *Kredit und Kapital*, *37*, pp. 329–352.

8 Comparative analysis of the operational efficiency of conventional and Islamic banks

1. Introduction

We assume that Indonesia's "neoliberal" regulatory framework did not improve the profitability and efficiency of its Islamic banks. To endorse this assumption, this chapter aims to measure and compare the efficiency of the conventional and Islamic banks in Indonesia using the non-parametric data envelopment analysis (DEA) method.

This chapter also reviews the studies on the efficiency of conventional and Islamic banks in Malaysia. We attempt to clarity the positive rent effect that Malaysia's Islamic banking industry has achieved which Indonesia's Islamic banking industry has not yet achieved. In doing so, this chapter purposes to partly answer Puzzle 2 – What were the secrets for the successful development of Malaysia's Islamic banking? – as well as testing Hypothesis 1: Indonesia's financial regulators (Bank Indonesia and the Financial Services Authority, FSA) failed to create an adequate incentive for Islamic banks in Indonesia, leading to a state failure of omission.

The rest of this chapter is organized as follows. Section 2 looks at the measurement of efficiency and DEA. Sections 3 and 4 explain the data and methodology used for our analysis of the efficiency of Indonesia's Islamic and conventional banks. Section 5 compares our results with the case of Malaysia, referring to the previous studies. Section 6 sets out the chapter summary.

2. The measurement of efficiency by data envelopment analysis (DEA)

Sastrosuwito (2012) underlines two approaches to efficiency measurement: "input-oriented" and "output-oriented". The input-oriented approach is focused on minimizing input as output is assumed to be fixed. In contrast, the output-oriented approach puts the effort in expanding the maximum output without altering the input used.

One of the key points for determining efficiency is "technical changes". The measurement of technical efficiency addresses technical and operational correlations in the process of converting inputs into outputs in a production process. It is considered that the technical change or technical efficiency would determine the "production frontier", which represents the maximum output possibly reached by using the available inputs. The frontier depends on the economies of scale and the technology level held in the business unit.

The applicability of the concept of production frontier to the banking industry entails further investigation. However, as Bauer et al. (1998) point out, many scholars and researchers look at the "efficiency frontier" or x-efficiency as a tool of comparing the performances of financial institutions. This approach measures the deviation that occurs between the performance of financial institutions and best practice, which reflects the efficient frontier under the assumption that the financial institutions face the same market conditions. The use of frontier efficiency is becoming more popular as the estimation of frontier efficiency uses the technique of programming or statistics to mitigate the bias possibly occurring in the process of production, and the other exogenous effects which would affect the benchmark estimation (Bauer et. al., 1998; Ascarya et al., 2009).

DEA has been developed and widely utilized as a tool for measuring the efficiency of the business unit based upon the non-parametric method. By using mathematical linear programming, DEA measures the relative efficiency level of a decision-making unit (DMU) against its equivalent DMU under the condition that all these units are at or below the efficiency curve (Jemric and Vujcic, 2002). The advantage of using DEA is that this approach does not require an explicit assumption in creating any efficiency frontier formula. In other words, DEA is a relative efficiency measurement tool that does not need a pre-considered functional structure requisite in the data to determine the efficient units (Ascarya and Yumanita, 2008; Avkiran, 2013). This is the advantage as well as the limitation of using DEA.

DEA is a non-parametric, deterministic method for determining the relative efficient production frontier, based on the empirical data of chosen inputs and outputs of DMUs. From the set of available data, DEA identifies the reference points (relatively efficient DMUs) that define the efficient frontier (as the best practice production technology) and evaluates the inefficiencies of other, inferior points (relatively inefficient DMUs) that are below the efficient frontier (Jemric and Vujcic, 2002). The efficiency of DMU is calculated under this equation:

$$\frac{\sum_{k=1}^{p} \mu_k \, y_{k0}}{\sum_{i=1}^{m} v_i \, x_{i0}}$$

Where:

DMU: decision-making unit

n: number of DMUs evaluated

m: different inputs

xij:	number of input *i* consumed by DMU*j*
p:	different outputs
ykj:	number of output *k* produced by DMU*j*

3. The measurement of Indonesian banks' efficiency

The banking industry is a sector that has a special character in its operation. The banking industry is different from the manufacturing industry in the aspects of its main business activities: it essentially carries out financial transactions and channels financial resources, often under conditions of clients' "risk" and "uncertainty", from the financial surplus unit to the deficit of financial units. Meanwhile, the manufacturing industry has a specification in its major activity to produce physical products using a number of raw material inputs in the production process (Sastrosuwito, 2012).

Studies that use the non-parametric DEA method to analyse the efficiency status of the banks in Indonesia are, among others, Hadad et al. (2008a; 2008b), Ascarya and Yumanita (2008), Ascarya et al. (2009), and Sastrosuwito (2012). Among the findings in the existing literature that concern us are that state-owned banks were the most efficient ones and the local banks were the least (Hadad et al., 2008a); and foreign-owned banks had less efficient levels compared to their domestic counterparts (Haddad et al., 2008b). According to Ascarya and Yumanita (2008), during the period of 2002 to 2005, Indonesia's Islamic banks were more efficient compared to Malaysia's Islamic banks in all three measurements: technical, scale, and overall efficiency – although this was not consistent with our hypothesis. According to Ascarya et al. (2009), during the period of 2002 to 2006, Indonesia's Islamic banks had a slightly higher level of efficiency compared to conventional banks in terms of scale, technical, and overall efficiency measurements. This is also not consistent with our hypothesis.

4. Methodology and data description

Basically, we followed the methodology adopted by Ascarya and Yumanita (2008) and Ascarya et al. (2009), with a slight modification. We assumed the outputs in conventional and Islamic banks to be the credit/financing channelled (y1), the total assets (y2), and the total revenue (y3). The bank intermediary inputs for this function are the total deposits (x1), the human resource expenses (x2), the interest/profit-and-loss-sharing expenses (x3), and the operational expenses (x4). In this research, we ignored the fixed asset variable as one of the inputs and made the total asset variable as one of the outputs in the calculation of the efficiency scale, to focus on elaborating the intermediation function of the banking business and to avoid the bias peculiar to the model of manufacturing industry production function.

We used the data of individual banks from their financial statements accessed from the website of the FSA and/or the annual reports published for the period of 2008 to 2014. The total number of sampled banks were 68 conventional banks and seven to 12 Islamic banks. The sample covered 68.1 per cent of the existing number of banks as of 31 December 2014.

5. Results and analysis

Our analysis suggests that during the observation period of 2008 to 2014, the efficiency levels of conventional banks were higher than those of Islamic banks in light of overall, technical, and scale efficiencies. It should be noted that, especially in the overall and scale efficiency measures, Islamic banks had a slightly declining trend of efficiency level in the period (Table 8.1). As for conventional banks, with regard to the overall efficiency measures, we find that, in general, their efficiency levels were stable during the period. In contrast, Islamic banks' efficiency levels were more fluctuating. In terms of overall efficiency measures, their levels were very volatile and had a declining trend with a range from 72 to 83 per cent. As mentioned, our result is not consistent with Ascarya et al.'s (2009) comparative study during the period from 2002 to 2006. In our analysis during the period of 2008 to 2014, however, it is apparent that most Indonesian Islamic banks suffered from lower levels of efficiency in comparison with conventional banks.

In our view, this lower-level efficiency performance of Islamic banks partly endorses the reason for the deterioration of Islamic banks' financial and operational performances in Indonesia during the period of 2005 to 2018, as discussed in Chapter 3. Higher non-performing financing and operating cost to operating income in Islamic banks during the period of 2008–2018 may be related to their lower efficiency in the technical as well as scale levels.

As pointed out by Yudistira (2004), who assessed the efficiency level of Islamic banks compared to their conventional bank counterparts in different countries during the period of 1997 to 2000, we may say that the differences in Islamic banks' efficiency levels were determined and explained by country-specific factors. Though the causal relation is not clear from the results, we assume that the oligopolistic market structure based upon the dominance by the big conventional banks in Indonesia and the intensified competition among Islamic banks

Table 8.1 Summary of non-parametric DEA efficiency levels

Efficiency measures	*2008*	*2009*	*2010*	*2011*	*2012*	*2013*	*2014*
Conventional banks:							
Overall technical efficiency	0.95	0.94	0.93	0.96	0.98	0.97	0.96
Pure technical efficiency	0.96	0.95	0.94	0.97	0.98	0.97	0.98
Scale efficiency	0.99	0.99	0.99	0.99	1.00	1.00	0.99
Islamic banks:							
Overall technical efficiency	0.83	0.75	0.65	0.71	0.69	0.72	0.78
Pure technical efficiency	0.91	0.88	0.81	0.87	0.89	0.91	0.93
Scale efficiency	0.91	0.85	0.82	0.82	0.79	0.81	0.84

Source: Constructed by the authors.

Table 8.2 Average efficiency scores of Malaysian banks in the period 2007–2010

Efficiency measures	*Average efficiency scores during the period 2007–2010*
Conventional banks:	
Overall technical efficiency	0.92
Pure technical efficiency	1.25
Scale efficiency	0.81
Islamic banks:	
Overall technical efficiency	1.14
Pure technical efficiency	1.49
Scale efficiency	0.88

Source: Constructed by the authors based on Mohamad and Said (2013, pp. 7–8).

(Chapter 7) may have hindered Islamic banks' opportunity to improve their scale and technical efficiencies. At least, we should not overlook the fact that Indonesian Islamic banks failed to catch up with conventional banks in their scale efficiency. This endorses our hypothesis that Indonesia's Islamic banks were not given the adequate rent opportunities to maintain their franchise value as prudent monitors; consequently, they failed to get a big enough profit base to expand their office-branch networks.

In contrast, despite the differences in their measurement method, Malaysia's Islamic banks have a higher efficiency in comparison with conventional banks (Yudistira, 2004; Sufian, 2006; Tahir et al., 2009). Several studies were conducted in measuring and analysing the efficiency levels in Islamic banks in Malaysia using the DEA method.

Mohamad and Said (2013) conducted an efficiency analysis of conventional and Islamic banks in Malaysia using the DEA method for the years from 2007 to 2010. Table 8.2 shows the calculated average scores in the technical and scale efficiencies of the Malaysian banks in this period. It is apparent that Malaysia's Islamic banks showed relatively higher scores in comparison with conventional banks in terms of pure technical efficiency. Also, in terms of scale efficiency, the Islamic banks indicated significantly higher achievements in comparison with conventional banks. Although the number of comparative studies on bank efficiencies is limited, it appears that the case of Malaysia is in sharp contrast to the case of Indonesia. We assume that the satisfactory level of scale efficiency achieved by Islamic banks is attributable to the Malaysian government's "centralized" initiatives for incubating the Islamic banking industry in Malaysia.

6. Summary

The main purpose of this chapter is to obtain relative efficiency performance levels between Islamic and conventional banks in Indonesia and Malaysia, based upon the DEA method. The results endorse our hypothesis. Malaysia's interventionist regulatory framework has brought a positive rent effect for its Islamic banks, improving scale efficiency together with technical efficiency. On the other hand, Indonesia's neoliberal regulatory framework has left its Islamic banks behind the dominant big conventional banks. Indonesian Islamic banks were not allowed to utilize the opportunity for leveraging the conventional infrastructure and networks. Apparently, Indonesia's neoliberal policy was harsh on its Islamic banks, and lost them the opportunity to seek enough scale efficiency to compete with conventional banks.

References

Ascarya and Yumanita, D. (2008) Comparing the efficiency of Islamic banks in Malaysia and Indonesia, *Buletin Ekonomi, Moneter dan Perbankan, 11*(2), pp. 95–119.

Ascarya, Yumanita, D., and Rohimah, G.R. (2009) Analisis efisiensi perbankan konvensional dan perbankan Syariah di Indonesia dengan Data Envelopment Analysis, in N. Huda. and M.E. Nasution (Eds) *Current Issues Lembaga Keuangan Syariah.* Jakarta: Prenada Media Group, pp. 1–36.

Avkiran, N.K. (2013) Bank efficiency measurement and network DEA: A discussion of key issues and illustration of recent developments in the field, in F. Pasiouras, (Ed.) *Efficiency and Productivity Growth: Modelling in the Financial Services Industry.* Singapore: John Wiley & Sons, pp.171–191.

Bauer, P.W., Berger, A.N., Ferrier, G.D., and Humphrey, D.B. (1998). *Consistency Conditions for Regulatory Analysis of Financial Institutions: A Comparison of Frontier Efficiency Methods. Financial Services Working Paper, 02/97.* Cleveland, OH: Federal Reserve Bank of Cleveland.

Hadad, M.D., Hall, M.J.B., Kenjegalieva, K., Santoso, W., Satria, R., and Simper, R. (2008a) Bank efficiency and stock market performance: An analysis of listed Indonesian banks, *Loughborough University Discussion Paper Series*, No. 7.

Hadad, M.D., Hall, M.J.B., Kenjegalieva, K., Santoso, W., Satria, R., and Simper, R. (2008b) Efficiency in Indonesian banking: Recent evidence. *Loughborough University Discussion Paper Series*, No. 13.

Jemric, I. and Vujcic, B. (2002) Efficiency of banks in Croatia: A DEA approach, *Comparative Economic Studies, 44*, pp. 169–193. doi: https://doi.org/10.1057/ces.2002.13

Mohamad, N.H. and Said, F.B. (2013) Performance analysis of conventional and Islamic banking in Malaysia using super efficient DEA model. Paper presented at *2013 SIBR Conference on Interdisciplinary Business and Economics Research*, Bangkok, 6–8 June 2013.

Sastrosuwito, S. (2012) Determinants and impact of bank efficiency on economic growth: Empirical evidence from Indonesia. Unpublished PhD dissertation, Ritsumeikan Asia Pacific University, Japan.

Sufian, F. (2006) The efficiency of Islamic banking industry in Malaysia: Foreign vs domestic banks, *Review of Islamic Economics, 10*(2), pp. 27–53.

Tahir, I. M., Abu Bakar, N.M., and Haron, S. (2009) Estimating technical and scale efficiency of Malaysian commercial banks: A non-parametric approach, *International Review of Business Research Papers, 5*(1), pp. 113–123.

Yudistira, D. (2004) Efficiency in Islamic banking: An empirical analysis of eighteen banks, *Islamic Economic Studies, 12*(1), pp. 1–19.

9 Structural dilemma of Indonesia's Islamic banking

1. Introduction

Indonesia's regulatory structure which underpins the Islamic banking industry is, in our view, inadequate for creating a good incubation process for the development of Islamic banks. This is reflected in the market and business structures which are not always conducive to Islamic banks: high entry barriers by the domination of conventional banks in the market; severe competition with conventional banks as well as among Islamic banks; lack of capability and capacity in credit risk management; and lower levels of efficiency and profitability. This is the structural problem which creates the deterioration of Islamic banks' financial and operational performance in Indonesia.

We witnessed that Indonesia's Islamic banks failed to optimize the rent effect (Hellmann et al., 1997) in the market as an adequate incentive to boost the development of Islamic banking. Despite the need for a structural reform in the Indonesian Islamic banking market to enhance its contribution to the economy, why was the structural reform not adequately processed? Economic and banking policies implemented by the government and financial authorities in Indonesia related to the development strategy of Islamic banks, to some extent, still nuanced "neoliberal" policy, by disregarding the importance of creating a "real" level playing field for an affirmative policy which should be favourable to incubating Islamic banking. This chapter proposes a theoretical framework for considering what may have prevented the structural reform in Indonesian Islamic banking. We hypothesize that Indonesia's decentralized or fragmented political structure may have interlocked with the structural dilemma of the extraordinarily low level of penetration of Islamic banking in Indonesia.

So far, we have referred to a unique "structural failure" regarding the inadequacies in the Islamic banking regulatory structure to incubate Indonesia's Islamic banks, which have resulted in their low level of penetration and the recent slowed-down growth of Islamic banking. Now, we should also refer to a unique "transition failure" – that is, the inadequacies in the pace and direction of institutional changes to achieve better efficiency over time have resulted in the failure of creating a level playing field between conventional and Islamic banks in Indonesia. Less has been addressed in the existing academic debate to this latter type of state failure (transition failure) in which Indonesia's Islamic banking is trapped.

The rest of this chapter is organized as follows. Section 2 attempts to point out the structural dilemma (structural and transition failures) in Indonesia's Islamic banking. Section 3 gives our concluding comments.

2. Understanding the structural dilemma of Indonesia's Islamic banking

As we discussed in Chapter 8, it is apparent that Indonesian neoliberal policy was harsh on its Islamic banks, and lost them the opportunity to seek out enough scale efficiency to compete with conventional banks. For those infant Islamic banks to catch up with conventional banks in Indonesia, the regulator should have considered creating the rent opportunities to be captured by Islamic banks to give them time for learning (rent for learning) or for improving the skills and capacity for screening and monitoring borrowers (management/monitoring rent).

On the other hand, rent opportunities for learning and for monitoring may become unproductive "monopoly" rent (Khan, 2000). In the initial stage of incubating the Islamic banking industry, some Indonesian Islamic banks might have desired to obtain a monopolistic rent upon their licence as *Shari'ah*-compliant financial lenders. In theory, if the regulator restricted the licence for dealing Islamic financial products only to the licensed Islamic banks, they would be in an advantageous position for keeping an effective power in the Islamic banking market if such a market exists, supported by many "*Shari'ah* loyalist customers". In reality, there were only a few *Shari'ah* loyalists in Indonesia: reportedly only 1 per cent of the population using the formal financial institutions. Under this circumstance, the regulator did not have to worry so much about the possibility of the occurrence of unproductive monopoly rent, even if a protective regulatory framework was installed.

As we discussed in Chapter 3, Indonesia's Islamic banks, in general, suffered from lower profitability, lower efficiency, thinner capital bases, higher cost of funds, and smaller office-branch networks than conventional banks. This harsh outcome for Islamic banks, under the neoliberal regulatory framework for encouraging free competition in the banking industry – a competition on two levels, between Islamic and conventional banks, as well as among Islamic banks – can be considered a unique structural failure, as the inadequacies in the Islamic banking regulatory structure for incubating Indonesia's Islamic banks resulted in Islamic banking's low level of penetration and recent slow growth (see Figure 9.1).

Our comparative study on the performance of Islamic and conventional banks in Indonesia, Malaysia, and Bangladesh (Chapter 6) suggests that especially low profitability, lower efficiency, and less stability in Indonesia's Islamic banks are rather peculiar to that country's case. The general inefficiency in operations and a seemingly underdeveloped skill in credit risk management in Indonesia's Islamic banks are observed. Why did Indonesia's Islamic banks alone fall into the trap?

Here, Khan's approach (1995, 2000) is helpful in describing the interaction between financial authorities and market players in rent-seeking. To answer the above question, we compared the regulatory framework in Indonesia with

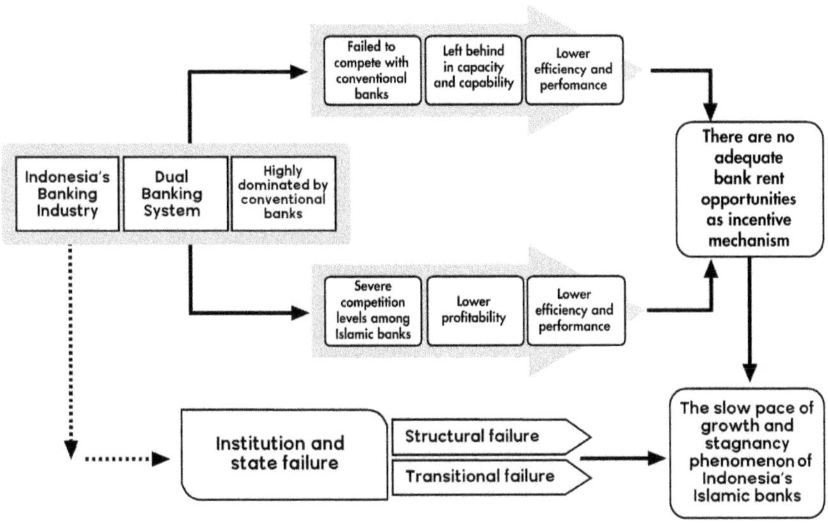

Figure 9.1 Structural dilemma underpinning the Islamic banking market.
Source: Constructed by the authors.

that in Malaysia (Chapter 5). As we pointed out, Malaysia's centralized (or top-down) approach to incubation of Islamic banking was reflected in its political patronage-client structure of promoting the government's preference for the economic interests of *Bumiputera* (ethnic Malay people), which is dominated by a Muslim population (see Haneef, 2001; Lai, 2015). In contrast, we can see a decentralized or fragmented political structure in Indonesia, which was reflected in the slow process of incubating its Islamic banking industry. This structure was partly underpinned by the influence on economic policy during the New Order period in 1966 to 1998 by the so-called Berkeley Mafia group in the Ministry of Finance (MOF) and the central bank, Bank Indonesia (BI). The widely known group, primarily influenced by an Anglo-American neoliberal school of economic thought, was positioned against the interventionist view (see Robison, 1990; Baswir, 2006).[1]

Even though the neoliberal regulatory framework is to be blamed, it led us to ask: Why didn't Indonesia change the framework? Even the latest *Roadmap of Indonesian Islamic Banking 2015–2019* (FSA, 2015) and *Roadmap of Indonesian Islamic Finance 2015–2019* (FSA, 2017) do not present a detailed policy direction in terms of market structure and incentive mechanisms for the enhancement of Indonesia's Islamic banking industry. This problem is related to transition failure. Transition failure refers to the inadequacies in the pace and direction of institutional changes to achieve better efficiency over time (Khan, 1995). In theory, Indonesia's transition cost must be high under a decentralized political structure. As we saw in Chapter 5, the lack of political leadership and the coordination problem among government agencies and financial sector authorities under a fragmented political structure in Indonesia, especially after the economic reform agenda since 1998, can be raised as the cause of the slow process in policy-making.

During the New Order government under President Suharto (1966–1998), the President and his ministers in the cabinet grasped the ruling power to coherently regulate all the industries, including the banking and finance sector, under a kind of authoritarian regime. In the development stage under the regime, the planning and coordination of regulations in the economic and financial sector was to some extent coherently implemented under the initiatives by the ministers in the national economic team, including BI. It was in 1998 when the authoritarian regime collapsed and was followed by the implementation of an economic and bureaucratic reform programme. This democratization progress was accompanied by a by-product: the fragmentation of the distribution of political bargaining power between the executive authority (the government) and the legislative (the parliament) in the process of making the economic and financial policy. This fragmented structure of political power may have hindered prompt and adequate planning and implementation. For instance, we highlight that an extraordinarily long process was undertaken until the enactment of Act No. 21 Year 2008 concerning Islamic Banking, which had been proposed in the House of Representatives (the parliament) in 2005 and finally ratified in 2008, which means that it took no less than approximately 16 years since the first Islamic bank was established in Indonesia in 1992 (Wibisono, 2009).

In the case of Malaysia, we observe that the development of Islamic banking and finance was attributable to the political initiative and partisanship in supporting its prompt incubation as an important political and economic agenda, appealed to by major political parties such as the United Malays National Organisation and Malaysian Islamic Party. The promotion of incubating and expanding the principles in the mode of Islamic banking and finance, in particular the prohibition of *riba*, was advocated by several political parties in the general election campaign so as to get support from their political constituents, especially from the *Bumiputera* voters (Lai, 2015). In contrast, the promotion and incubation of its Islamic banking and finance was not often used as a campaign in the political arena in Indonesia. As a result, it seems that neither the executive nor the legislative bodies faced any strong pressure from their political constituents to promptly incubate Indonesia's Islamic banking and finance. As an example of the slow process of decision-making, we can raise the response to the controversial case of double tax imposition on *murabaha* transactions. In fact, it took around 17 years since the establishment of the first Islamic bank in 1992 to finally abolish the double tax imposition for *murabaha* transactions in Islamic banking operations, with the enactment of Act No. 42 Year 2009 on Tax Neutrality.

Additionally, we should take note of a potential coordination problem among the governmental agencies. On the one hand, this may be reflected partly in the Indonesian political way or behaviour of seeking for a consensus. On the other hand, certain rent-seeking and compromise among them may have lost the coherence in the governmental policies and regulations related to Islamic banking and financial institutions.

Upon the enactment of Act No. 21 Year 2011 concerning Financial Services Authority (FSA) on 17 October 2011, the FSA was initiated as the new supervisory authority for the banking and financial industry in Indonesia from 31 December 2013. The FSA was expected to become the main banking supervisory authority in Indonesia. In fact, it was expected to take the full range of responsibility for supervising not only the banking sector, but also non-bank financial institutions, and capital market and micro-finance institutions, except for the micro-finance sector under the cooperative legal entities. However, it is said that the FSA often faces a coordination problem with other governmental agencies related to economic and Islamic financial affairs, including BI, the National *Shari'ah* Board, the Ministry of Religious Affairs, the Directorate General of Taxes and Fiscal Policy Agency under the MOF, and the Ministry of Cooperatives and Small and Medium Enterprises. The fragmented structure with several heads may have increased the burden of coordination, consequently preventing the FSA from initiating the comprehensive and coherent regulatory arrangements for the development of Islamic banking and financial institutions.

An example of the burden in coordination is the controversy of the so-called "spin-off" requirement. Upon Act No. 21 of 2008 regarding Islamic Banking article 68 paragraph 1, a type of conventional bank with Islamic banking windows is required to perform the spin-off accomplishment of its Islamic windows to become a fully-fledged Islamic bank, when: (1) the *Shari'ah* business unit through the Islamic banking windows has reached 50 per cent of the assets of its parent conventional bank; or (2) 15 years will have passed since this Act took effect (by the end of July 2023 at the latest). The FSA has been engaged in implementing the spin-off regulation, a requirement that is still controversial among major stakeholders of the Islamic banking industry. For instance, most Islamic bankers and the Indonesian Islamic Banking Association insist that the deadline for the conversion to fully-fledged Islamic banks should be suspended, taking into account the expected significant impact on the operation of the converted banks. Probably, the FSA is facing the burden of coordinating the public interest sought in the House of Representatives and the stakeholders of Islamic banking. If the FSA compromises with the latter, the amendment of Act No. 21 Year 2008 will be scheduled in the parliament, which would be time-consuming. Besides, the FSA will have to pay the extra "transaction cost" for coordinating with BI if a synergy enhancing the stability of a payment system is pursued by the spin-off requirement, as well as with the MOF if this policy needs a fiscal and taxation incentive package to ease the burden in the process of spin-off and conversion.

3. Concluding comments

Despite very significant discussions in the literature on the institutional specificities of Indonesian Islamic banking, less has been done to investigate the reason why the regulations on Islamic banking resulted in poor outcomes for Indonesia's

Islamic banks. In this chapter, we drew on the institutional approach by Khan (1995, 2000) to observe the process and pace of institutional (governmental) failure in adequately creating and modifying the structure for the development of Indonesian Islamic banks. We proposed a view that Indonesia's Islamic banking industry has been trapped into a structural dilemma and hypothesized that Indonesia's decentralized and fragmented political structure is reflected in this dilemma. We have to admit that this view entails further testing and discussion.

Note

1 We perceive that the Berkeley Mafia group played a strategic role and became an economic architect, in particular, in the New Order government under the late President Suharto. In the economic reform era since 1998, the technocratic group that controlled economic and financial policies in the government, especially at the MOF and BI, had, in our view, been influenced by neoliberal schools of economic thought. These technocrats are the proponents of such neoliberal economic thought which, with the free-market doctrine, is in certain aspects characteristic of what is commonly known as the "Washington Consensus" dictum (see Chang and Grabel, 2004; Wibisono, 2007).

References

Baswir, R. (2006) *Mafia Berkeley dan Krisis Ekonomi Indonesia.* Yogyakarta: Pustaka Pelajar.

Chang, H.-J. and Grabel, I. (2004) *Reclaiming Development: An Alternative Economic Policy Manual.* London and New York: Zed Books.

Financial Services Authority (FSA). (2015) *Roadmap of Indonesian Islamic Banking 2015–2019 (Roadmap Perbankan Syariah Indonesia 2015–2019).* Jakarta: FSA, Republic of Indonesia.

Financial Services Authority (FSA). (2017) *Roadmap of Indonesian Islamic Finance 2015–2019 (Roadmap Keuangan Syariah Indonesia 2015–2019).* Jakarta: FSA, Republic of Indonesia.

Haneef, M.A. (2001) Islam and economic development in Malaysia – A reappraisal, *Journal of Islamic Studies, 12*(3), pp. 269–290.

Hellmann, T., Murdock, K., and Stiglitz, J. (1997) Financial restraint: Toward a new paradigm, in M. Aoki, H.-K. Kim, and M. Okuno-Fujiwara (Eds) *The Role of Government in East Asian Economic Development: Comparative Institutional Analysis.* Oxford: Clarendon Press, pp. 163–207.

Khan, M. (1995) State failure in weak states: A critique of new institutionalist explanations, in J. Harriss, J. Hunter, and C.M. Lewis (Eds) *The New Institutional Economics and Third World Development.* London: Routledge, pp. 71–86.

Khan, M. (2000) Rents, efficiency and growth', in M. Khan and J.K. Sundaram (Eds), *Rents, Rent-seeking and Economic Development: Theory and Evidence in Asia.* Cambridge: Cambridge University Press, pp. 21–69.

Lai, J. (2015) Industrial policy and Islamic finance, *New Political Economy, 20*(2), pp. 178–198.

Robison, R. (1990) *Power and Economy in Suharto's Indonesia.* Manila: The Journal of Contemporary Asia Publishers.

Wibisono, Y. (2007) Reformasi ekonomi: Apa dan mengapa, *INDIE Review*, *7*(II), pp. 7–12.

Wibisono, Y. (2009) Politik ekonomi UU perbankan Syariah peluang dan tantangan regulasi industri perbankan Syariah, *Bisnis dan Birokrasi, Jurnal Ilmu Administrasi dan Organisasi*, *16*(2), pp. 105–115.

10 Hypothesis explaining the low penetration of Indonesia's Islamic banks

Shari'ah-compliant benchmark and *Shari'ah*-based *raf' al-haraj* benchmark on prohibition of *riba*[1]

1. Introduction

> "Allah has imposed no hardship (*haraj*) upon you in religion"
>
> (Holy Qur'an, Al Hajj: 78).

One of the salient features of Islamic finance that distinguishes it from the conventional financial model is that the former complies, in objectives and operations, with *Shari'ah* (Islamic law). Prohibition of *riba* (interest) is one of the major prohibitions in *Shari'ah* principles. The Holy Qur'an (Al Baqarah: 275–276) clearly states that dealing with *riba* – profit on loans – is "sinful". However, it is still difficult to get explicit Qur'anic text on the logic as to why interest is prohibited because the rationales are more implicit than explicit. Islamic scholars, for instance, Siddiqi (2004), in analysing the context of various Qur'anic verses summarize five broader reasons: (1) interest corrupts society; (2) interest implies improper appropriation of others' property; (3) interest slows down the growth of real sectors; (4) interest demeans and diminishes human personality; and (5) interest is simply unjust. Although the Qur'an does not provide detailed analysis of the rationale of prohibition of interest, the only rationale in regard to the prohibition of *riba* that can be sensed from Qur'anic verse is related to "exploitation" or "injustice" (Suzuki and Miah, 2018; p. 14). As stated in the Qur'an, "deal not unjustly (by asking more than your principal) and you shall not be dealt with unjustly" (Al Baqarah: 279).

In general, the profit on sales has no ceiling, and may be determined by market competition or technology. If we assume that *murabaha* is trade, the associated profit also should have no limit. Meanwhile, in conventional finance, "usury" is prohibited. Usury is referred to as a rate of interest greater than that which the law or public opinion permits (Looft, 2014). For instance, in Japan, the law prohibits the lender operating as a business unit to form any contract to receive an annual interest exceeding 20 per cent. The lender that breaches the law is subject to imprisonment with work for not more than five years, a fine of not more than 10 million yen, or both. This leads us to ask a question: How is the Islamic lender prohibited from charging a profit margin in the (*Shari'ah*-compliant) *murabaha* transaction greater than that which is equivalent to the "usury" referred to in conventional finance? This point is understated in academic as well as practitioners' debate in Islamic finance.

Here, we propose to set up two benchmarks to judge whether a particular financial transaction is acceptable or not in the context of Islamic finance: a "*Shari'ah*-compliant" benchmark and a "*Shari'ah*-based" *raf' al-haraj* (removal of hardship) benchmark. The former benchmark is addressed to ensuring that a transaction brings "profit on sale", not "profit on loans". The latter benchmark should be addressed to ensuring that a transaction does not exploit anyone. Perhaps, most Islamic scholars may wish to believe that these two benchmarks are identical in a sense that *Shari'ah*-compliance would bring the desired outcome towards social justice. However, even in the *Shari'ah*-compliant *murabaha* transaction, the lender is still able to exploit the borrower by pricing an extraordinarily high mark-up, resulting in unnecessary hardship for the borrower.

In the framework of the Islamic jurisprudence principle (*ushul fiqh*), Al-Zuhaili (1979) admits that Islamic law is built with a number of characteristics that form the basis of the development of the norm of law, namely, *al-taisir* (lightening), *al-tashiil* (easing), *al-samahah* (tolerance), *al-i'tidaal* (moderation), and *raf 'al- haraj wa al-masyaqqah* (removal of hardship and incrimination).

It is worth noting, according to Imam Malik, one of the great thinkers in Islamic law (711–793 CE), that the concept of benefit or interest of the public (*mashlahah mursalah*) in implementing Islamic law lies in its aim to maintain a primary necessity (*dharurii*) and removal of hardship (*raf 'al-haraj*) by incrimination (*masyaqqah*) and harm (*madharaat*) (Al-Syatibi, 1999).

Focusing on the removing of hardship (*raf 'al- haraj*) principle for example, it is possible that we will find some "misleading impact" on society, as contradictions that deserve our concern are encouraged in the Holy Qur'an:

> "Allah has imposed no hardship (*haraj*) upon you in religion" (Al Hajj: 78)
> "Allah does not burden a soul beyond its capacity" (Al Baqarah:286)
> "Allah desires not to inflict any hardship upon you" (Al Maidah: 6)

Intrinsically, it is arguable that the "imperative spirit" of Islamic financial transactions does not exploit anyone. Consequently, we may identify *taysir* (ease) and *raf' al-haraj* (removal of hardship) as objectives (*maqashid*) rather than rules of specific application. Making things easier for people and removing unnecessary hardship from them are among the cardinal objectives of the *Shari'ah*, and these principles tend, in many ways, to characterize Islam itself (Kamali, 2000).

> This is because each is inherently dynamic and comprehensive, and tends to involve a process capable of continuous application and refinement. In this sense the two principles are as relevant to the conditions of society today as they were in the early days of Islam.
>
> (ibid., p. 70)

2. Instrumental rationality and procedural rationality

This issue may be related to the debate on "instrumental rationality" and "procedural rationality" in social philosophy. Our economic activities are subject to our bounded rationality because we do not have absolute existence with omniscience and omnipotence, but are human beings with brains of limited computational capacity. In order to get closer to the Truth, it is quite rational for believers to give their best effort in the exercising of *ijtihad* to understand and incarnate the logic and rationales implicit in the Qur'anic text. This exercise of *ijtihad* can be treated as being "instrumentally" rational for getting closer to the Truth. On the other hand, our behavioural patterns aim to be instrumentally rational at the beginning. However, as more complex factors are encountered, the patterns would quite often change to be limitedly instrumental, eventually become "procedurally" rational at best.

According to Weales (1992; pp. 62–65), *homo sociologicus* is introduced in the process of investigating how the freedom of manoeuvre might be bounded by the preference of others. In particular, this introduces constraints on human action through norms. The associated sociological concept of a role shows how *homo sociologicus* is educated from childhood to adulthood, thereby encoding norms and conformity to norms into roles that become immediate motives of behaviour. Norms make the calculation tasks easier, but actions based on prevalent social norms will typically be difficult to justify in terms of instrumental rationality. If all individuals reason in a role- or rule-bounded way, their collective action may fail to achieve, and certainly to maximize, individual and collective benefit (see also Suzuki, 2011; pp. 26–27).

Instrumental rationality can be matched with *Maqashid al Shari'ah*. Islamic banks must not only follow the *Shari'ah* principles in terms of compliance to Islamic principles in structuring their business contracts as the legal system of pragmatism and convenience, but they should also uphold the guiding spirit of *Maqashid al Shari'ah*. From an Islamic economic perspective, *maqashid* can be observed in two dimensions: the *Shari'ah* (law) and the objective of *mukallaf* (being religiously responsible or accountable). Obviously, most Islamic banks comply with *Shari'ah*. However, they have to reflect the spirit of *Shari'ah* on their performance by striving to achieve justice, equity, and fairness. As Dusuki and Abozaid (2007; p. 144) state, "the values which prevail within the ambit of the *Shari'ah*, are expressed not only in the details of its transactions, but also in the breadth of its role in realizing the *Maqashid al Shari'ah*".

On the one hand, it is quite meaningful to exert the best effort to try to understand the real reasons and logic behind the prohibition of *riba* in the Qur'anic text. On the other hand, merely trying to meet the way of *Shari'ah* compliance without seeking its rationale can be construed as procedural rationality. The *Shari'ah*-compliant benchmark is a necessary condition, but not always a sufficient condition. Transactions in Islamic finance should be monitored not only for *Shari'ah* compliance, but also for *Shari'ah*-based circumstances. Unlike conventional banks, the maxim of profit maximization alone is unsuited to *Maqashid al Shari'ah*, but rather, profit should be accompanied by justice and fairness at all levels of human interaction (Chapra, 2000). In this sense, Islamic banks must not exploit their customers, either *ex-ante* or *ex-post*. It is, however, difficult to provide rigorous empirical evidence on the compliance of *Maqashid al Shari'ah* because the literature is very scarce on the issue.

3. *Shari'ah*-compliant *murabaha*

Murabaha is the dominant mode of finance of Islamic banks across the world. The term *murabaha* refers to a particular kind of sale. Unlike ordinary sales, the seller in *murabaha* transactions discloses the real cost of the object offered for sale to the buyer and adds a certain profit above the cost price. Thus, *murabaha* is known as a marked-up sale. The mark-up may be a lump sum amount or based on a percentage. In *murabaha* transactions, the buyer can make the payment on the spot or on a subsequent date agreed upon by the parties.

There is serious debate as to whether a *murabaha* or mark-up transaction really complies with Islamic principles. The debate stems from the fact that the mark-up or the extra charge above the cost price is pre-fixed, which is akin to conventional bank lending. Since the profit earned from *murabaha* is certain and pre-fixed, some Islamic economists criticize *murabaha* for simply being a conventional banking product under the guise of an Islamic name. In this commercial transaction of Islamic banks, profits are made from sales, which are allowed, whereas profits on loans are unlawful. Thus, even if it is sometimes ambiguous whether *murabaha* falls into the profit-and-loss-sharing (PLS) category, it is considered a *Shari'ah*-compliant product (Miah and Suzuki, 2018).

The term *Shari'ah*-based is referenced by Çizakça (2011). According to him:

> To the extent that modern Islamic finance is not built directly from the *Shari'ah* (*Shari'ah* based approach) but rather form the Islamically modified conventional banking (*Shari'ah* compliant approach), the result is high costs, low profits and most importantly, a dilution of respectability.
>
> (ibid., p. 3)

The essence of the *Shari'ah*-based approach is the realization that "there is a substantial difference between the Western *homo-economicus*, the rational man, who has discarded all religious and ethical teachings and acts purely to maximize his profits but does so subject to the laws and ethics of Islam" (ibid., p. 5). Apparently, Çizakça is very concerned about the pure mode of PLS as a fundamental element for realizing *Shari'ah*-based Islamic finance, so he criticizes the dominance of *murabaha* finance in the credit portfolio of Islamic banks as a *Shari'ah*-compliant but less *Shari'ah*-based syndrome.

As supported by a *fatwa* issued by Majd al-Din 'Azzam, in his capacity as Advisor to the International Union of Islamic Banks, it appears that there is a consensus to see that "an exchange of money for money based on the sale of a commodity of which the buyer becomes the owner once he/she assumes liability for the payment of its price" does not fit the definition of *riba* (Kamali, 2000; p. 174). On the other hand, besides Çizakça's (2011) benchmark on whether it falls into the pure PLS mode, it appears that there is not yet a consensus on how to define *riba* in the context of the objectives (*maqashid*) of the *Shari'ah*. Taking into consideration the dominance of the *murabaha* contract in Islamic finance, it is not enough to criticize the *murabaha* syndrome just because the contract is not in the pure mode of PLS. Rather, *murabaha* finance should be encouraged, unless it breaches the *maqashid – raf' al-haraj* circumstances – of the *Shari'ah*.

4. Role of competition with conventional financiers

The issue is how the regulators in Islamic finance set up the ceiling rate of profit for pricing *murabaha* finance by the regulated Islamic financiers, so as to not make them exploit their clients. However, to the best of our knowledge, we could not find any specific clause on the ceiling profit rate in any guidelines for Islamic finance being prepared by the regulatory authorities, nor by the central *Shari'ah* board, to prevent Islamic financiers from enjoying excessive profit from their clients. Perhaps, there may be two arguments that Islamic financiers could put forward in favour of their position. One is that they have to compete with conventional financiers in the same market; and another is that there is no clear-cut *fatwa* against this practice.

Usury is prohibited in conventional financial institutions (Looft, 2014). As mentioned earlier, in Japan the law prohibits the lender operating as a business unit to form any contract to receive an annual interest exceeding 20 per cent. In theory, insofar as a free and fair competitive market between Islamic and conventional financiers is being operated, any Islamic lender would not charge a profit margin in a *murabaha* transaction greater than that which is equivalent to the usury referred to in conventional finance, because any higher profit margin would not attract their clients to enter into any contract of *murabaha*. In other words, the prohibition of usury in conventional financial institutions would be influential, at least "indirectly", on Islamic financiers as an important regulation for preventing them from exploiting their clients. For instance, in Bangladesh, as one of the Muslim countries, "usurious" loans are regulated to give additional powers to courts to deal with certain cases with usurious loans of money or in kind (the Usurious Loans Act, 1918 (Act No. X of 1918) in Bangladesh).

Even in Muslim countries, the term usury is empirically used as a completely unacceptable or illegal transaction. For instance, in Indonesia, a business based on *Shari'ah* principles is regulated as a business which does not contain, including but not limited to, the elements of usury, *maisir*, *gharar*, *haram*, and *zalim*[2] (Article 2, Elucidation to the Act of the Republic of Indonesia Number 21 of 2008 concerning *Shari'ah* Banking). Here, usury is defined as

> illegally obtained additional income (*batil*), among others the exchange transaction of similar types of goods but of different quality, quantity, and delivery time (*fadhl*), or in lending transaction requiring the Facility

Receiving Customer to repay the fund received exceeding the principal due to the passing of time (*nasi'ah*)[3].

Since the above regulation in Indonesia does not refer to *riba*, the received demarcation between *riba* and the usury mentioned appears vague. However, it is apparent that usury here, in referring to *batil*, *fadhl*, and *nasi'ah*, is understood as an unacceptable and illegal transaction based upon "opportunism". In general, opportunism in terms of pursuing self-interest with guile involves subtle forms of deceit and refers to the incomplete or distorted disclosure of information, especially in calculated efforts to mislead, distort, disguise, obfuscate, or otherwise confuse (Williamson, 1985; p. 47). While profit on loans (*riba*) is prohibited, the usury based upon opportunistic behaviours is also prohibited in Islamic banking in Indonesia (from another perspective, we wonder if there might be a "grey zone", where usury without or with fewer opportunistic elements would be acceptable as a customary practice or a necessary evil). However, the definition of usury in the regulation is too ambiguous to judge how the Islamic lender is prohibited from charging a profit margin in the *Shari'ah*-compliant *murabaha* transaction greater than that which is equivalent to the usury referred to in conventional finance.

Indonesian Islamic banks rely for their funding sources mainly on time deposits, savings accounts, and current accounts. As we saw in Chapter 3, their costs of funds stay not lower than those of conventional banks, despite the operations of Islamic banks being exposed to a higher liquidity risk and potential displacement risk. In the period 2008–2018, the cost of savings accounts for Islamic banks was in a range between 2.1 and 5.7 per cent, while it was from 1.3 to 3.1 per cent for conventional banks. The cost of current accounts for Islamic banks was between 0.7 and 2.2 per cent, and 2.1 and 2.9 per cent for conventional banks. And the cost of time deposits for Islamic banks was between 5.1 and 8.6 per cent, while it was from 5.6 to 10.7 per cent for conventional banks. In general, the costs of current savings accounts and time deposits for Indonesia's Islamic banks tended to be higher than conventional banks, except for equivalent rates for time deposits by Islamic banks in the years 2008, 2013, and 2018.

However, as we also observed in Chapter 3, the lending rate to their customers offered by Indonesia's Islamic banks remains not lower than that of conventional banks. Our observation on the equivalent rates of lending of Islamic banks in comparison with the lending rates of conventional banks in the period of 2008–2018 shows that the rate for working capital of Islamic banks was in the range between 12.8 and 19.3 per cent, while it was 10.4–14.6 per cent for conventional banks. The rate for investment by Islamic banks was 11.7–18.0 per cent and 10.4–14.0 per cent for conventional banks. Consumption by Islamic banks was 10.6–14.3 per cent while it was 11.7–15.8 per cent for conventional banks. Taking into consideration the overall rate of growth or gross domestic product in Indonesia, the lending rates offered by both types of banks tend to stay at the level which may have repressed the general economic activities by their customers. In this context, we would say that the pricing rate offered by Islamic banks to their customers

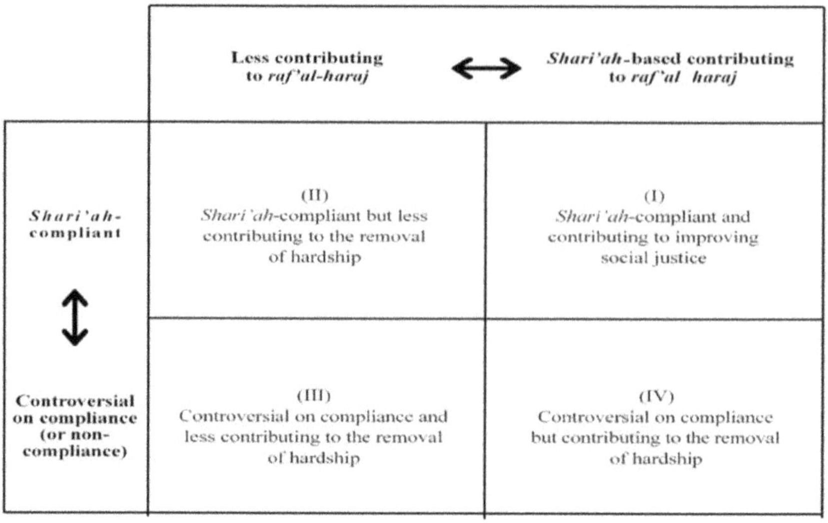

Figure 10.1 Categories of grey zones in Islamic finance.
Source: Constructed by the authors.

did not always contribute to *raf' al-haraj*. At the same time, we should note that the attractive rate in consumption financing through *murabaha* contracts, due to their higher cost of funds, may have squeezed the profit opportunity to be captured by Indonesia's Islamic banks, which may not encourage them to penetrate further into the business of consumption financing.

Figure 10.1 shows the categories of "grey zones" in Islamic banking in different combinations of *Shari'ah*-compliant and *Shari'ah*-based *raf' al-haraj* benchmarks. The net social benefit would be the highest in quadrant I, where Islamic financiers are contributing well to the removal of hardship in borrowers based upon *Shari'ah* compliance. In quadrant II, Islamic financiers are complying with the *Shari'ah*, but contribute less to the removal of hardship in borrowers. From the perspective of Islamic "perfectionist" economists who respect the pure mode of PLS, the so-called *murabaha* syndrome could be considered to fall into this quadrant. (Nevertheless, as mentioned earlier, we support the Islamic "realist" view. For instance, Bakar (2016) gives a warning that while Islamic economists advocate "wealth distribution", they are forgetting a much more important element, which is "wealth creation". We categorize the *Shari'ah*-compliant *murabaha*, if it is still contributing to the removal of hardship in borrowers through the function of wealth creation, as a contract in quadrant I.)

Quadrant II suggests a grey zone. If Islamic financiers obtain a profit margin in the *Shari'ah*-compliant transaction greater than that which is equivalent to the usury referred to in conventional finance, the transaction with the excess rate of profit would be considered as "usurious trade" that exploits the borrowers.

Meanwhile, the opportunity of charging a high, but socially permissible, profit margin or less usurious trade may create a grey zone in the quadrant that contributes less to the removal of hardship in borrowers. Quadrant III is the worst contract; it is either controversial in terms of *Shari'ah* compliance or non-compliance, while contributing the least to the removal of hardship in borrowers. The transactions in this quadrant – most likely based upon opportunism – are difficult to be justified, turning out to be "black".

Figure 10.1 suggests one other grey zone in Islamic finance. In quadrant IV, the transactions or contracts that Islamic financiers offer are still controversial in terms of *Shari'ah* compliance, but they are contributing to the removal of hardship in borrowers through the function of wealth creation. We may recall the issue of *tawarruq*, which is prohibited in Indonesia; most scholars, particularly in Indonesia, believe that the transaction of *tawarruq* is not *Shari'ah*-compliant. We can say that the quadrant IV-type grey zone in Indonesian Islamic banking seems narrower, partly undermining the profit base for Islamic banks in Indonesia. Yet in Malaysia, this category of grey zone can be considered to be wider in creating and maintaining a level playing field between conventional and Islamic banks.

Should the above mentioned grey zone in quadrant IV be allowed to enable Islamic banks to charge a higher margin to the extent permitted by public opinion? The allowance may be related to the profitability of Islamic banks. This view may provide us with a bold hypothesis that explains the market penetration levels by Islamic banks in Indonesia and Malaysia. Indonesia is the most populous Muslim country in the world. In 2010, the total population of Indonesia was estimated at 204.8 million people and the Muslim proportion was about 88.1 per cent (Pew Research Center, 2011). Indonesia is expected to become a magnet for the development of Islamic banking and financial markets. However, Indonesia's Islamic banks still occupy a very marginal market share; as at the end of June 2018, they were recorded to comprise about 5.7 per cent of the national banking industry. Compared to the Islamic banking penetration in Malaysia, which holds 26.5 per cent of market share, the level of Islamic financial deepening in Indonesia is remarkably low (IFSB, 2019).

We hypothesize that Indonesian Islamic banks are not given an adequate incentive (including the financial sector rent opportunity) to contribute to Islamic financial deepening. Owing mainly to the severe competition with conventional banks (as well as among Islamic banks) in the industry, Indonesia's Islamic banks cannot afford to earn sufficient profits for maintaining their franchise value and reputation (Suzuki et al., 2017), compared to the situation of Islamic bank rent opportunities available in the banking sector of Malaysia. As we observed in Chapter 6, in order to compare the performance of the Islamic banks and the banking sector as a whole, the return on assets (ROA) of Indonesia and Malaysia during the period 2007 to 2015 were scrutinized. It is shown that the ROA of the Islamic banking sector in Malaysia was almost the same as that of the overall banking sector. In contrast, the ROA of the Islamic banking sector in Indonesia was consistently lower than that of the conventional banking sector during the whole of this period (please refer to our statistical data and discussion in Chapter 6). This implies that the Indonesian banking regulator(s) failed to incubate Islamic banks by giving them the learning rent opportunity or designing a level playing field between conventional and Islamic banks in an appropriate timeframe; while the Malaysian regulators did these successfully, although the rationale behind the protective framework for Malaysian Islamic banks should entail further clarification.

Another hypothesis is that the grey zone provided for Indonesia's Islamic banks is not as wide as that for Islamic banks in Malaysia. For instance, while the contract of *tawarruq* (reverse *murabaha*) is allowed in Malaysia, it is not allowed in Indonesia. In this contract, the buyer buys an asset from a seller (usually from a bank) at a cost-plus basis on a deferred payment system. The buyer then sells the same asset to a third party (the bank which usually manages the sale) on a cash basis. The buyer basically borrows cash from the second transaction and pays the original seller the instalment or lump sum payment owed. This sort of transaction is controversial, because the intention of the commodity purchases is not for the buyer's use or ownership (Miah and Suzuki, 2018). The width of grey zones might be different in each country.

5. Can "usurious trade" be prohibited?

Apparently, the more problematic grey zone – though a certain width might be necessary for Islamic banks in the stage of incubation – is the quadrant II type. Particularly in the Marxian tradition of viewing economic activities through a "class struggle", lending money at interest without any means of sharing risk between lender and borrower creates a relationship where weak and vulnerable individuals can be easily exploited by more powerful ones. In theory, if negotiation and contracting between lender and borrower were monitored by society or the community (*ummah*), the opportunity to be exploited would be less.

By differentiating trade from usury, the Qur'an reaffirms the practice of trading as a respectable profession (Looft, 2014). The issue is, however, whether we have to consider the possibility of "usurious trade". Upon the element of asymmetric information, fraud, no-confidence, and distrust between counterparties, a trade party could possibly be exploited. The potential usurious trade should be prohibited in the context of *raf' al-haraj*, the removal of hardship, as the cardinal objective (*maqashid*) of the *Shari'ah*. As Hazik and Hassnian (2019) point out, the democratization of formal financial services is indeed crucial for the economic empowerment of the Muslim *ummah*, or the general public. If usurious trade is to be prohibited, the usurious pricing on the *murabaha* contract by Islamic financiers should be prohibited, too. The principle of prohibition of *riba* should be argued, not only from the *Shari'ah*-compliance viewpoint, but also based on the *Shari'ah raf' al-haraj* benchmark; that is, in the context of prohibition of exploitation for realizing social justice for the benefit of the general public.

At the same time, we should not overlook the fact that a certain width of grey zone might be necessary to incubate Islamic financiers who would contribute to the community through their function of mediating financial resources.

Simultaneously, we should note that enough inducement to invest (creation of effective demand through investment or governmental expenditure or export) to achieve full employment in society might be a pre-condition for realizing the Islamic mode of PLS, accordingly realizing the prohibition of *riba,* including the prohibition of usurious profit. Perhaps we may say that Indonesia faces a difficulty in finding an appropriate width of grey zone for incubating its Islamic banking.

6. Concluding comments

Based on our discussion above, we would like to put forward some concluding comments on the issue. First, Islamic scholars and the main *fatwa* authorities in Indonesia, namely Lajnah Bahsul Masa'il, Nahdlatul Ulama, Lembaga Tarjih, Muhammadiyah, and the Indonesian *Ulama* Council (Majelis Ulama Indonesia/MUI), have played a strategic role in fostering the growth and development of Indonesia's Islamic banking and finance industry in the past three decades. This is particularly marked in their contribution to issuing and disseminating the *fatwa* on the prohibition of bank interest. However, this official *fatwa* of prohibition of *riba* should also take a stand, not to disregard the basic principles of Islamic law in making it easier (*taysir*), but to remove unnecessary hardship (*raf' al-haraj*) for the people.

Second, we should note that the pricing rate offered by Indonesian Islamic banks is, in general, relatively high compared to conventional banks. In particular, we can see the tendency of high pricing in consumption financing through *murabaha* contracts (this financing is dominant in their credit portfolios) as well as in the two-step financing by Islamic banks in Indonesia. We are concerned about the possibility that Indonesia's Islamic banks might have neglected the *raf' al-haraj* principle for their customers.

Third, there is room to discuss the phenomenon of the low penetration of Indonesia's Islamic banks from a hypothetical perspective, in that Indonesia might be trapped in a "diminishing equilibrium" between *Shari'ah* compliance and the *Shari'ah*-based *raf' al-haraj* benchmark. It is a great challenge for the proponent of Islamic banking to seek out a certain width of grey zone to best incubate Islamic financiers who would contribute to the community by mediating more financial resources, while simultaneously seeking an optimal equilibrium for enhancing the net social benefit, whereby Islamic banks make great contributions to the removal of hardship for their customers based upon *Shari'ah* compliance.

Notes

1 This chapter is reproduced from Yasushi Suzuki (2019) "Riba, usury and Keynes", *Islam Civilisation and Renewal, 10*(2), pp. 175–188, and Yasushi Suzuki and Mohammad Dulal Miah (2020) "Shari'ah-compliant benchmark and Shari'ah-based 'raf' al-haraj' benchmark on prohibition of riba", *International Journal of Islamic and Middle Eastern Finance and Management* (forthcoming). We are grateful to the International Institute

of Advanced Islamic Studies, Malaysia, and Emerald Publishing Limited, UK, for consenting to our reproduction.

2 In short, these terminologies can be defined as follows: ***maisir*** is "a transaction depending on unstable conditions and on luck"; ***gharar*** is "a transaction of which the object is not clear, not owned, not known in terms of its whereabouts, or cannot be delivered at the time of transaction unless otherwise regulated in *Shari'ah*"; ***haram*** is "a transaction of which the object is prohibited in *Shari'ah*"; and ***zalim*** is "an unfair transaction for the other party".

3 In the Act of the Republic of Indonesia No. 21 of 2008, the word "usury" is used to translate the word ***riba***. It seems that the choice of the word usury instead of "interest" in translating the word *riba* implies that there is still a debate and controversy as to whether or not bank interest is the same as *riba* and is accordingly prohibited in Islam (see our discussion in Chapter 2). It is worth noting that all of the three main *fatwa* authorities in Indonesia – Lajnah Bahsul Masa'il, Nahdlatul Ulama; Lembaga Tarjih, Muhammadiyah; and MUI – have put in place public benefit (***maslahah***) as an essential indicator in implementing Islamic law for society. In particular, although MUI has issued the *fatwa* on prohibition of bank interest, it also comes with the exception that, for areas which are not yet covered by Islamic bank services, it is still permissible to use conventional bank services based on the necessity principle (***dharuriyah***) or reasons. Obviously, MUI in its purpose of enacting the *fatwa* on prohibition of bank interest has had a profound consideration on the principle of primary necessity (***dharuriyah***) and hardship removal (*raf' al-haraj*) as a foundation in implementing Islamic law.

References

Al-Syatibi, A.I. (1999) *Al-Muwaffaqât fi Ushûl al-Syarî'ah*. Beirut: Dâr al-Ma'rifah.

Al-Zuhaili, W. (1979) *Nazhâriyyah al-Dharûrah al-Syar'iyyah*. Beirut: Muassasah al-Risâlah.

Bakar, M.D. (2016) *Shariah Minds in Islamic Finance*. Kuala Lumpur: Amanie Media.

Chapra, M.U. (2000) *The Future of Economics: An Islamic Perspective*. Leicester: The Islamic Foundation.

ÇizakÇa, M. (2011) *Islamic Capitalism and Finance: Origins, Evolution and the Future*. Cheltenham, UK: Edward Elgar.

Dusuki, A.W. and Abozaid, A. (2007) A critical appraisal on the challenges of realizing Maqasid Al-Shariah in Islamic banking and finance, *International Journal of Economics, Management and Accounting, 15*(2), pp. 143–165.

Hazik, M. and Hassnian, A. (2019) *Blockchain, Fintech, and Islamic Finance*. Berlin: DejG Press.

Islamic Financial Service Board (IFSB). (2019). *IFSB's Islamic Financial Services Industry (IFSI) Stability Report 2019*. Kuala Lumpur: IFSB.

Kamali, M.H. (2000) *Islamic Commercial Law*. Cambridge: The Islamic Texts Society.

Looft, M. (2014) *Inspired Finance*. Basingstoke, UK: Palgrave, Macmillan.

Miah, M.D. and Suzuki, Y. (2018) A critique to a naïve critique to "Murabaha" "tawarruq" syndrome, in Y. Suzuki and M.D. Miah (Eds) *Dilemmas and Challenges in Islamic Finance*. Abingdon, UK: Routledge, pp. 28–44.

Pew Research Center. (2011) The future of the global Muslim population: Projections for 2010–2030. Retrieved from http://assets.pewresearch.org/wpcontent/uploads/sites/11/2011/01/FutureGlobalMuslimPopulationWebPDF-Feb10.pdf

Siddiqi, M.N. (2004) *Riba, Bank Interest and the Rationale of Its Prohibition.* Jeddah, Saudi Arabia: Islamic Research and Training Institute (IRTI).

Suzuki, Y. (2011) *Japan's Financial Slump: Collapse of the Monitoring System under Institutional and Transition Failures.* Basingstoke, UK: Palgrave Macmillan.

Suzuki, Y. and Miah, M.D. (2018) Heterodox vs Islamic views on interest and uncertainty, in Y. Suzuki and M.D. Miah (Eds), *Dilemmas and Challenges in Islamic Finance.* Abingdon, UK: Routledge, pp. 11–27.

Suzuki, Y., Uddin, S., Pramono, S., and Khan, S. (2017) Islamic bank rent: Comparison among Bangladesh, Indonesia, Malaysia, and Pakistan, in Y. Suzuki, M.D. Miah, M.K. Wanniarachchige, and S.M.S. Uddin (Eds) *Banking and Economic Rent in Asia: Rent Effects, Financial Fragility, and Economic Development.* Abingdon, UK: Routledge, pp. 121–137.

Weales, A. (1992) Homo Economicus, Homo Sociologicus, in S. Hargreaves Heap et al. (Eds) *The Theory of Choice: A Critical Guide.* Oxford: Blackwell, pp. 62–72.

Williamson, O.E. (1985) *The Economic Institutions of Capitalism.* New York: The Free Press.

11 Epilogue

A quarter-century journey of Islamic banking development in Indonesia

1. Summarized conclusions

Having passed a quarter-century journey of Islamic banking development in Indonesia since its first establishment in 1992, it is high time to review the *raison d'être* of Islamic banks and their role in the Indonesian economy. Indonesia is the most populous Muslim country in the world. Taking into account also its endowments and potential of economic resources, the Islamic banking industry in Indonesia was expected to play an important role in facilitating more financial resources and in contributing as a magnet to the internationalization of the Islamic mode of financing, particularly in the Asia-Pacific region. However, the reality is far from the expectation. This book aimed to solve the following puzzles:

- Puzzle 1: Even though Indonesia has the largest Muslim population, and despite the fact that regulatory initiatives have been implemented for the purpose of facilitating the Islamic banking industry, why is the Islamic financial deepening (the market share of Islamic banks) extraordinarily low so far? What has caused the recent trend of slow-paced Islamic financial deepening? How is this phenomenon related to trends in contemporary Islamic banks' performance on operational efficiency?
- Puzzle 2: Why has Indonesia failed to catch up with Malaysia, a close neighbouring Muslim country that has somewhat successfully proceeded with the Islamization of its own banking industry? What were the secrets for the successful development of Malaysian Islamic banking? How well (or poorly) can Malaysia's Islamic financial architecture be applied to Indonesia? From another perspective, how do the stakeholders of Islamic banks in Indonesia (especially the Financial Services Authority, Bank Indonesia (the central bank), the government of Indonesia, the bankers themselves) interact and resolve the structural dilemma faced by the Indonesian Islamic banking industry? How did they fail to manage the market and institutional/state failures aligned with the process of the Islamization of the banking industry under the dual banking system?

This book analysed the economic reality behind the extraordinarily low level of Islamic financial deepening in Indonesia, a share of no more than 6 per cent. Our investigation clarified how Indonesia's Islamic banks suffered from lower profitability, lower efficiency, thinner capital bases, higher cost of funds, and smaller office-branch networks than conventional banks. This structural problem may have undermined the profit base for Islamic banks and lost them their edge to compete with conventional banks. We assumed that this situation led to the slow-paced growth of the Islamic banking industry since 2012.

We looked at the important role of financial sector rent as the incentive for banks to mediate financial resources (to reduce credit rationing under the imperfect information paradigm). The bank rent opportunity can function as the rent for learning to catch up and improve skills and capacity for credit risk management. This book clarified how the Indonesian regulator(s) failed to institutionalize a profit base for incubating Indonesia's Islamic banks by giving them an appropriate incentive to become prudent fund providers/monitors, ideally while complying with *Shari'ah* rules. Rather, the government of Indonesia has encouraged the free and competitive credit market among conventional and Islamic banks. We pointed out that if the Islamic bank rent hypothesis is held, the governmental neoliberal policy would tend to dwarf the Indonesian Islamic banking industry.

This book compared the Indonesian regulatory framework with that of Malaysia. We were concerned that Indonesia's Islamic banking was unsuccessful in implementing the strategic programme in massively opening the Islamic banking windows/divisions to leverage the conventional banking infrastructure. This was in sharp contrast to the case of Malaysia. We found that Indonesia's Islamic banks were not given an adequate tax and fiscal incentive even in the early stages of their incubation. This was also in a sharp contrast with the case of Malaysia. These findings prove that the Indonesian financial authorities failed to create the rent opportunities to be captured by Islamic banks for sufficiently learning the skills and knowledge in credit risk monitoring to compete with conventional banks.

Compared to the cases of Malaysia and Bangladesh, we found that Indonesia's Islamic banking slump – especially its lower profitability, lower efficiency, and less stability – was rather peculiar to the case of Indonesia. We pointed out that the higher ratio of operating expenses to income was not attributable to the exposure of "hands-on" equity-like financing, because the nature of the *musharaka* financing adopted by Indonesia's Islamic banks was not a type of purely "participatory" financing. We analysed the general inefficiency in operations and the seemingly inadequate skills in credit risk management in Indonesia's Islamic banks, especially in managing their *mudaraba* and *musharaka* financing portfolios.

We analysed Indonesia's credit market structure, the concentration over time, and competition configuration, to highlight how Indonesian Islamic banks were facing a more severe competition with conventional banks, as well as among themselves, in the banking industry. We pointed out that the two-fold unfavourable conditions experienced by Islamic banks – the dominant presence by the big three or five commercial banks in the banking sector and the intensified competition among Islamic banks, especially since 2012 – has been the reason for their lag in capability and competency; and worsening profitability performances have become the catalyst for their lower levels of efficiency and performance. Hence, this book suggests that the case of Indonesia's Islamic banks would support the competition-inefficiency hypothesis.

This book compared relative efficiency-performance levels between Islamic and conventional banks in Indonesia and Malaysia using the data envelopment analysis method. The results endorsed our hypothesis. Malaysia's "interventionist" regulatory framework brought a positive rent effect to its Islamic banks to improve their scale efficiency, together with their technical efficiency. On the other hand, Indonesia's neoliberal regulatory framework left its Islamic banks behind the dominant big conventional banks. This book provided a number of theoretical and empirical evidence to prove that this typical market-oriented and neoliberal financial policy lost Indonesia's Islamic banks the opportunity to seek out enough scale efficiency to compete with rival conventional banks.

Even though the neoliberal regulatory framework is to be blamed, it led us to ask: Why didn't Indonesia change the framework? This book suggested that Indonesia has been trapped into a "transition failure", which refers to inadequacies in the pace and direction of institutional changes to achieve better efficiency over time. We pointed out that the lack of political leadership under a fragmented political structure in Indonesia can be raised as the cause of the slow process in its policy-making and changes.

2. Proposed policy options and implications

Basically, the infrastructure of Islamic finance is necessary for facilitating the investment and economic transactions of Muslim depositors and investors. If the infrastructure is not available, they would have to pay more transaction costs for *Shari'ah* compliance at individual level. If they are aware (or unsure) that the proceeds from their investment had not complied with *Shari'ah* principles, some Muslim investors would consider that their proceeds should be "purified", for instance, by being donated to charity or *zakat* institutions. This circumstance may discourage them to engage in investment. In other words, developing an infrastructure for Islamic finance would possibly mobilize more funds from Muslim investors, which would also contribute to national economic growth. The governmental initiatives for developing this infrastructure are expected to reduce the seemingly high transaction costs for *Shari'ah* compliance at individual level in Indonesia. This is not only beneficial for Muslim investors, but also for society, because if more funds from Muslim investors are mediated for investment, they would contribute to the growth of the nation.

We assume that the overall stagnated development of Indonesia's Islamic banking was attributable to the government's failure to create a profit base for Islamic banks to develop their skills and capacity for managing their credit portfolios. The existing governmental banking policy should be critically assessed from the perspective of incubating the Islamic banking industry in Indonesia. However, if the Islamic bank rent hypothesis holds – that is, Islamic banks must earn more profit than conventional banks, to create and maintain their franchise value as *Shari'ah*-compliant prudent monitors – we should ask how difficult would it be, under the free and competitive market, for Islamic banks to create a reputation as prudent fund providers, especially under *mudaraba* and *musharaka* financing contracts upon the mode of profit-and-loss sharing.

Our argument in this book provides a number of theoretical and empirical evidence to prove that the stereotypical neoliberal regulatory framework of seeking a "nominal" level playing field in the overall banking industry would hamper the growth of Islamic banking. Basically, our argument may support an "affirmative" action in favour of incubating Indonesian Islamic banking. This is, of course, subject to the condition that the enhancement of Islamic banking is expected to contribute to macroeconomic growth and the improvement of quality of life for all in the nation.

Several scholars have contested some affirmative policies for the development of Indonesia's Islamic banking (for instance, Ismal, 2013; Bustaman, 2014; Bappenas, 2015). Their proposals are summarized as follows:

(1) *Conversion of one of the leading state-owned conventional banks into a fully-fledged Islamic bank.*

 Looking at the seemingly oligopolistic banking structure occupied by the top five commercial banks (including state-owned ones; see the related discussion in Chapter 7), privatization per se is justifiable (if the rent-seeking cost from the opponents does not exceed the expected benefit for society from the privatization). The converted bank is expected to capitalize on the scale and technical efficiency accumulated, as a leading commercial bank, to contribute to setting up a "real" level playing field for Islamic and conventional banks.

(2) *Give more opportunities for Islamic banks to engage in large-scale infrastructure projects under guarantee by the government.*

 The opportunities are expected to help the development of the *musharaka* (equity-like participatory) financial market and *sovereign sukuk* bond market.

(3) *Give the licence of undertaking the* ummah *savings fund for* Hajj *(the Pilgrim to Mecca) only to Islamic banks.*

 This would give a rent (profit base) to Islamic banks while justifying their *raison d'être*. Besides, the financial authorities should encourage the Islamic financial institutions to be involved more in managing the investment portfolios of *Hajj* funds, hence giving them the opportunity to acquire the skills and knowledge of adequate fund and risk management.

(4) *Establish a specialized Islamic bank based upon the governmental initiatives.*

 In this proposal, a governmental or government-led Islamic bank is established as a specialized bank to mediate financial resources using the Islamic mode of financing, for instance, to small- and medium-sized enterprises or start-up companies with great potential. The accumulated skills and knowledge in credit risk management are expected to be transferred to private Islamic banks in the long run. Perhaps, Islamic banks can contribute to incubating the *halal* industry and to financially supporting the

Muslim lifestyle, including *halal* food and Muslim fashion, which have enormous demand in the Muslim world.

Undoubtedly, the affirmative policies should be carried out meticulously by the government. To some extent, the expansion of the Islamic banking infrastructure would mobilize funds from the "second-tier" *Shari'ah* loyalists. In an economic sense, the feasibility of the mentioned affirmative action may depend on the size of these second-tier loyalists in Indonesia. Besides, we should ask: Who could initiate the policies under conditions of higher transition cost in this country? While it is important to learn the lessons from the Malaysian government's initiatives for incubating Islamic banking, we should note that it is intrinsically difficult for Indonesia to copy Malaysia's political structure, which enables the Malaysian government to implement centralized regulation. Needless to say, while a "decentralized" political structure would face higher transaction costs for coordination and decision-making, centralized state intervention would often amount to a risky strategy for giving bias by discouraging private initiatives in the market.

It is probably not only the government that is to be blamed for the slow process in policy-making. It appears that the top executives of Indonesia's Islamic banks might have lost their motivation for expanding their operations. Through our interviews with the bank managers of Indonesia's Islamic banks, we found in some cases the lack of a "strong will" from the top executives in seeking a synergized vision with conventional bank managers in attaining growth in Islamic banking. Without real demand from the "bottom", nothing would happen. Moreover, the lack of a strong will may lose Islamic banks the challenge to invest in new trends of financial technology ("fintech"). According to Dietz et al. (2016) in *McKinsey & Company Financial Services Insights*, the banks which do not mitigate the impact of "fintech risk" in their retail-banking business will increase the burden of risk on their revenue by 10–40 per cent by 2025.

Going back to the Islamic bank rent hypothesis (i.e. Islamic banks must earn more profit than conventional banks in order to create and maintain their franchise value as *Shari'ah*-compliant prudent monitors), we must say that it is extremely difficult for Islamic banks under the "free and competitive market" to cement their reputation as prudent fund providers. In Chapter 10, we shed light on the phenomenon of low penetration of Indonesia's Islamic banks from a hypothetical perspective, in that Indonesia might be trapped in a "diminishing equilibrium" by their *Shari'ah* compliance. To some extent, we expect that new IT technologies would help the supervising of *fatwas* and *Shari'ah* in Islamic finance institutions to reduce the transaction costs for *Shari'ah* compliance. Simultaneously, we expect that the effective governance of *fatwa* and *Shari'ah* supervision will be promoted by the conducive process of *ijtihad* (reinterpretation of contextual Islamic law) to avoid the trap of diminishing equilibrium (Bakar, 2016; Suzuki et al., 2018).

The Islamic mode of finance is expected to contribute not only to facilitating material prosperity, but also to enhancing people's quality of life and realizing social justice. We should recall the suggestion by Prof. M. Umer Chapra, a prominent scholar in Islamic economics, that Islamic economics is expected to not only be "maximizing economic growth, wealth and consumption", but also to contribute to establishing "a society where material prosperity is also accompanied by spiritual advance, human brotherhood, family and social harmony, social-justice and the well-being of all" (Chapra, 2000, p. 357). Some scholars expect the potential of *zakat*, *waqf*, and *sukuk* funds, which would contribute to coordinating a "blended finance", to have an element of social finance to alleviate poverty while sustaining development programmes in Indonesia (Muljawan and Kashoogie, 2016; IICPSD and IRTI-IDB, 2017). However, without the development of Islamic banking as the core of the Islamic mode of finance, their expectation might be just a dysfunctional chimera.

Again, we wish to reiterate that the governmental initiative for developing the infrastructure of Islamic finance and, in particular, Islamic banking, is not only beneficial for Muslim investors, but also for society, because if more funds from the Muslim investors are mediated for investment, they would also contribute to the growth of the nation. We should not leave Indonesia's Islamic banks as redundant financial institutions. While it may cause a controversy, we propose that leadership in implementing an economic and adequate affirmation policy from the financial authorities is a necessary condition, although we are not sure whether it is a sufficient condition at this point for incubating and developing the Islamic banking industry in Indonesia, or for turning Indonesia into an international Islamic financial hub in the Asia-Pacific region. This revisited journey hopefully conveys a moment for contemplation, as beautifully described in the Holy Qur'an, chapter Al Baqarah: 148: "Every nation has a direction (or vision) toward which it turns; you, therefore, try to excel in all that is good".

References

Badan Perencanaan Pembangunan Nasional (Bappenas). (2015) *Masterplan Arsitektur Keuangan Syariah Indonesia*. Jakarta: Bappenas.

Bakar, M.D. (2016) *Shariah Minds in Islamic Finance*. Kuala Lumpur: Amanie Media.

Bustaman, H. (2014) *Review on Indonesian Islamic Banks. A Classic Small Bank's Trap: Merger or Closure?* Material Presentation at ISEFID Forum, Jakarta, on 29 October 2014.

Chapra, M.U. (2000) *The Future of Economics: An Islamic Perspective*. Leicester: The Islamic Foundation.

Dietz, M., Khanna, S., Olanrewaju, T., and Rajgopal, K. (2016) Cutting through the noise around financial technology, *FinTechnicolor: The New Picture in Finance. McKinsey & Company Financial Services Insights*, pp. 6–14. Retrieved from: https://mck.co/33rvx4Q

Ismal, R. (2013) *Islamic Banking in Indonesia: New Perspectives on Monetary and Financial Issues*. Singapore: John Wiley and Sons.

Istanbul International Center for Private Sector in Development, United Nations Development Programme (IICPSD) and Islamic Research and Training Institute, Islamic Development Bank (IRTI-IDB). (2017) *I for Impact: Blending Islamic Finance and Impact Investing for the Global Goals*. n.p.: IICPSD and IRTI-IDB. Retrieved from: https://irti.org/product/i-for-impact-blending-islamic-finance-and-impact-investing-for-the-global-goals-2/

Muljawan, D. and Kashoogie, J. (2016) A new stage of development for Islamic economics and finance in Indonesia, in Islamic Research and Training Institute, Islamic Development Bank (IRTI-IDB), Thomson Reuters, and the General Council for Islamic Banks and Financial Institutions (CIBAFI). *Indonesia Islamic Finance Report: Prospects for Exponential Growth*. n.p.: IRTI-IDB, Thomson Reuters, and CIBAFI, pp. 88–90. Retrieved from: https://ceif.iba.edu.pk/pdf/ThomsonReuters-IndonesiaIslamicFinanceReportProspectsforExponentialGrowth.pdf

Suzuki, Y., Pramono, S., and Sahroni, O. (2018) Anatomy of governance structure in the mode of Islamic finance: An emphasis on the governance over Shari'ah boards, in Y. Suzuki and M.D. Miah (Eds), *Dilemmas and Challenges in Islamic Finance*. Abingdon, UK: Routledge, pp. 147–162.

Index

For Product Safety Concerns and Information please contact our EU representative GPSR@taylorandfrancis.com
Taylor & Francis Verlag GmbH, Kaufingerstraße 24, 80331 München, Germany

www.ingramcontent.com/pod-product-compliance
Ingram Content Group UK Ltd.
Pitfield, Milton Keynes, MK11 3LW, UK
UKHW011019180926
475701UK00004B/836
9780367644512